A
CONVERSATION
WITH A CAT

And Others

———

HILAIRE BELLOC

A
CONVERSATION
WITH A CAT

AND OTHERS

Essay Index Reprint Series

BOOKS FOR LIBRARIES PRESS
FREEPORT, NEW YORK

First published in 1931 by Harper & Brothers,
New York and Cassell & Co Ltd, London

Reprinted 1969 by arrangement with A. D. Peters & Co., Literary Agents

STANDARD BOOK NUMBER

8369-0035-9

LIBRARY OF CONGRESS CATALOG CARD NUMBER

69-18920

53, 748

PRINTED IN THE UNITED STATES OF AMERICA

To

J. B. MORTON

CONTENTS

A

CONVERSATION
WITH A CAT

And Others

ᴁ Conversation with a Cat

THE other day I went into the bar of a railway station and, taking a glass of beer, I sat down at a little table by myself to meditate upon the necessary but tragic isolation of the human soul. I began my meditation by consoling myself with the truth that something in common runs through all nature, but I went on to consider that this cut no ice, and that the heart needed something more. I might by long research have discovered some third term a little less hackneyed than these two, when fate, or some good influence or accident, or the ocean and my fostering star, sent me a tawny, silky, long-haired cat.

If it be true that nations have the cats they deserve, then the English people deserve well in cats, for there are none so prosperous or so friendly in the world. But even for an English cat this cat was exceptionally friendly and fine—especially friendly. It leapt at one graceful bound into my lap, nestled there, put out an engaging right front paw to touch my arm with a pretty timidity by way of introduction, rolled up at me an eye of bright but innocent affection, and then smiled a secret smile of approval.

No man could be so timid after such an approach as not to make some manner of response. So did I. I even took the liberty of stroking Amathea (for by that name did I receive this vision), and though I began this gesture in a respectful fashion, after the best models of polite deportment with strangers, I was soon lending it some warmth, for I was touched to find that I had a friend; yes, even here, at the ends of the tubes in S.W. 99. I proceeded (as is right) from caress to speech, and said, "Amathea, most beautiful of cats, why have you deigned to single me out for so much favour? Did you recognise in me a friend to all that breathes, or were you yourself suffering from loneliness (though I take it you are near your own dear home), or is there pity in the hearts of animals as there is in the hearts of some humans? What, then, was your motive? Or am I, indeed, foolish to ask, and not rather to take whatever good comes to me in whatever way from the gods?"

To these questions Amathea answered with a loud purring noise, expressing with closed eyes of ecstasy her delight in the encounter.

"I am more than flattered, Amathea," said I, by way of answer; "I am consoled. I did not know that there was in the world anything breathing and moving, let alone one so tawny-perfect, who would give companionship for its own sake and seek out, through deep feeling, some one companion out of all living kind. If you do not address me in words I know the reason and I commend it; for in words lie the seeds of all dissension, and love at its most profound is silent. At least, I read that in a book, Amathea; yes, only the other day. But

I confess that the book told me nothing of those gestures which are better than words, or of that caress which I continue to bestow upon you with all the gratitude of my poor heart."

To this Amathea made a slight gesture of acknowledgment—not disdainful—wagging her head a little, and then settling it down in deep content.

"Oh, beautiful-haired Amathea, many have praised you before you found me to praise you, and many will praise you, some in your own tongue, when I am no longer held in the bonds of your presence. But none will praise you more sincerely. For there is not a man living who knows better than I that the four charms of a cat lie in its closed eyes, its long and lovely hair, its silence, and even its affected love."

But at the word affected Amathea raised her head, looked up at me tenderly, once more put forth her paw to touch my arm, and then settled down again to a purring beatitude.

"*You* are secure," said I sadly; "mortality is not before you. There is in your complacency no foreknowledge of death nor even of separation. And for that reason, Cat, I welcome you the more. For if there has been given to your kind this repose in common living, why, then, we men also may find it by following your example and not considering too much what may be to come and not remembering too much what has been and will never return. Also, I thank you, for this, Amathea, my sweet Euplokamos" (for I was becoming a little familiar through an acquaintance of a full five minutes and from the absence of all recalcitrance), "that you have reminded me of my youth, and in a sort of shadowy

3

way, a momentary way, have restored it to me. For there is an age, a blessed youthful age (O My Cat) even with the miserable race of men, when all things are consonant with the life of the body, when sleep is regular and long and deep, when enmities are either unknown or a subject for rejoicing and when the whole of being is lapped in hope as you are now lapped on my lap, Amathea. Yes, we also, we of the doomed race, know peace. But whereas you possess it from blind kittenhood to that last dark day so mercifully short with you, we grasp it only for a very little while. But I would not sadden you by the mortal plaint. That would be treason indeed, and a vile return for your goodness. What! When you have chosen me out of seven London millions upon whom to confer the tender solace of the heart, when you have proclaimed yourself so suddenly to be my dear, shall I introduce you to the sufferings of those of whom you know nothing save that they feed you, house you and pass you by? At least you do not take us for gods, as do the dogs, and the more am I humbly beholden to you for this little service of recognition—and something more."

Amathea slowly raised herself upon her four feet, arched her back, yawned, looked up at me with a smile sweeter than ever and then went round and round, preparing for herself a new couch upon my coat, whereon she settled and began once more to purr in settled ecstasy.

Already had I made sure that a rooted and anchored affection had come to me from out the emptiness and nothingness of the world and was to feed my soul henceforward; already had I changed the mood of long years and felt a conversion towards the life of things, an appreciation, a cousinship with the created light—and all that through one new link of loving kindness —when whatever it is that dashes the cup of bliss from the lips of mortal man (Tupper) up and dashed it good and hard. It was the Ancient Enemy who put the fatal sentence into my heart, for we are the playthings of the greater powers, and surely some of them are evil. "You will never leave me, Amathea," I said; "I will respect your sleep and we will sit here together through all uncounted time, I holding you in my arms and you dreaming of the fields of Paradise. Nor shall anything part us, Amathea; you are my cat and I am your human. Now and onwards into the fullness of peace."

Then it was that Amathea lifted herself once more, and with delicate, discreet, unweighted movement of perfect limbs leapt lightly to the floor as lovely as a wave. She walked slowly away from me without so much as looking back over her shoulder; she had another purpose in her mind; and as she so gracefully and so majestically neared the door which she was seeking, a short, unpleasant man standing at the bar said, "Puss, Puss, Puss!" and stooped to scratch her gently behind the ear. With what a wealth of singular affection, pure and profound, did she not gaze up at him, and then rub herself against his leg in token and external expression of a sacramental friendship that should never die.

On Dressing Up

SURELY a burst and even an orgy of dressing up is a sign of vigour and of something to console any man for the declining age in which we live, and the collapse of culture and taste.

Boy Scouts, Girl Guides, A.A. Men, Doctors of Music in their robes, Chancellors, Yachtsmen, the Hunters of the Fox, and all the rest of them, pass by me in procession as I write. So do the new habits of ecclesiastical freakishness which so many deplore. It used to be a reproach against one community of amateur celibates that they dressed up their cook in a garb modelled upon an old print of a green and red gown worn in some Abyssinian monastery. But for my part, I praise the Prior or Precentor or Prebend or Archimandrite or whatever he may have called himself, who dressed up his dependent in this fashion. He also was for diversity; he also was for the need of colour, and for experiment in individualities, and the creative thing.

I praise also that man whose custom it was to denounce the legal profession (at whose hands he had suffered many things) by parading up and down the sea-front of a watering-place in Sussex thus accoutred:

6

he would dress entirely in black, with a long frock coat; on his head was a top-hat, nearly half as high again as that worn in those days (I am speaking of the years before the war) by the wealthier classes, as also by those less wealthy who buried the dead. Upon this hat he had pasted a large white paper band, which went all the way round and came nearly to the top of it, and had printed on it in huge letters "Avoid the Law."

Upon his back and upon his front he carried two huge cardboards, also white, and suspended over his shoulders by strings, as though he had been a sandwich-man. The one at the back held a simple curse against lawyers in general; the one in front went with some detail into his own particular grievance. Artistically, this last was a mistake, for no one could stop to read the number of words it contained. But the general effect was striking, and it was a noble instance of dressing up. So, in a lesser way, were the nigger minstrels on the beach. So (though nobody knew it but myself) was the very wicked old man who posed as an old salt, and dressed in the most exaggerated Drury Lane fashion, with bell-bottomed trousers, jersey and bare feet, to keep up that pretence, but who was, God knows, nothing more than a longshoreman with a great dread of the sea.

In one department, indeed, the glory of dressing up has diminished, but only in one. And that department is the one where formerly it had most scope, and sometimes ran riot. I mean the noble profession of arms. To-day all uniforms are similar enough. They have derived from Britain the belt and the puttee, and khaki for many, grey and horizon blue for others; but all, whatever their design, are designed for concealment, and are more uniform than uniforms should be.

What a splendid picture gallery the old uniforms make in the long years between the generation when Gustavus Adolphus hit upon the happy idea of clothing his men alike, so that he could tell which were his own men in battle, down to the Great War! Every service delighted in changing and re-changing the main type; and side by side with this main type, within each national group, there was a foison of invention. There was your Hussar coat with an empty sleeve hanging loose, and your Sabretache, and your Shako, and your headgear of which I do not know the name, but which had a sort of lining hanging out sideways loosely; and your varied helmets and cuirasses; and your blue belt and buckskin breeches and all. And then there were your red coats and your green coats and your purple, blue, white (as of the French Household Troops), and even mauve; and your black facings, and your yellows, and your creams, and your millinery shopfittings galore; and your epaulettes, and your myriad brass buttons which buttoned nothing (but there the boy in buttons beat the soldier), and your huge bearskin hat to terrify the foe; and your spurs, both gilt and plain. I suppose in the whole history of the human race there has never been such a multiplicity of design in the covering of the human body as that with which the various Ministers of War endowed the garrisons of Europe between the campaign of Lutzen and the Battle of the Marne.

This love of dressing up is a department, but the most vivid, the most innocent, in the great domain of Lying. The human love of a lie which colours all history and makes society what it has always been, the passion for unreality, the escape from things as they are, is to be marked and loudly praised in every function of life. It has given us polite manners, the whole vast structure of fiction in prose and verse, hero worship, myth, legend, diplomacy, high statesmanship and the ritual of Courts, whether martial or of justice, the rules of evidence (and of perjury), the systems called "philosophies" during the last hundred and fifty years, and the whole majestic science or art of history.

But nowhere does this necessity for the unreal, this thirst for what is not, this passion for falsehood, show more openly than in dressing up. How wrong are foreigners to blame the horsehair wigs of our advocates, judges and clerks! How wrong are puritans to be shocked at the surplice, let alone the cope or even the biretta; how much more I blame them for deriding mitres! With what pleasure do I not look upon the brimless hats of the Orthodox clergy, the green turban of the man who has made his pilgrimage to Mecca, the gaiters of the English bishop, the flaming red of the Cardinal, the purple of the Domestic Prelate, the various habits of the various Orders.

There are those who find cause for merriment, I for solemn gratitude, in the Ku-Klux-Klan, all dressed in night-gowns tied up like extinguishers over their heads, with ghastly slits for eyes, as also in the similar covering of the Brothers of the Misericordia, or the novel uniforms of those who meet in long white garments with crosses of red crimson sewn thereon, and in this fashion vow to defend Christian society against Bolshevism. And talking of Bolshevism, what better piece of dressing up than the hideous helmets of the Red soldiery; unless it be the gas mask of scientific war?

Nor let me forget the diver's dress, the New London County Council Scavengers' invented in the time of the Boer War (with their South African slouch hat neatly pinned up on the left side), and policemen of every grade.

When it was rumoured some months ago that wicked men had designs to undermine society by taking away the helmets of the London policemen and dressing them in caps, the argument then used to defeat this revolutionary intent was the necessity for protecting the policeman's head from blows. It was a false, utilitarian argument. The true foundation for preserving the London policeman's helmet is patriotism and the love of ancient things and the symbol of untruth, for in their helmets policemen inspire dread.

Shall I mention postmen, customs-house officials, the conductors of omnibuses, the varied and variegated staff of a railway company, the lift boys, the commissionaires? Shall I (as Cicero was wont to ask rhetorically before proceeding to answer his own questions)? No (as Cicero was wont to add, after having answered them). I will cut short my category, lest it should become infinite. We may have sacrificed, to our shame, the manifold diversity of the armed man in his dressing up, but we have amply made up for it in civilian life.

May the flood grow in volume as it proceeds. To the trained nurses and the policewomen, may there be added a special costume for every lady, denoting her titular rank—if she has one—her club, her association,

her fanaticism, and even—if it be not too much to hope
—let there be some growing diversity for us poor men.
I had a friend (now dead) who gave in my hearing
the truest political argument I have ever heard. He
gave it in a lowered voice to an American many years
ago at the Bar of the House of Lords. The visitor de-
plored (for he was of that philosophy) the artificial
barriers of rank and the signs of them. But my friend
said to him: "May the day come when every peer shall
wear his coronet round his hat in the streets!" And he
said that he, for his part, would be glad; for all such
things enhancing the multiplicity of life are something
done in the image of God's own action upon his creation. Yes, even as it is, with peers and baronets and
broad-arrow convicts and all, we have not come near to
the birds and the beasts and the beetles in multiplicity
of aspect. And what about the lilies of the field?

★ III ★

The Sources of the Seine

I HAVE during my life practised upon occasion the ritual of drinking from the sacred springs of rivers. The lesser rivers I so despise that unless they have some special sanctity about them, like the River Arun, or the River Ribble, I would not trouble to drink of their sources; for I do not think that these small fry can communicate any great virtue, even to their worshippers. I have therefore, of the smaller rivers, drunk only of the head springs of the River Arun, just above the lake where it rises; and though it was but a quarter of a mile off a road when I first traced it on a map, and though I go by that road often enough, I never deigned to drink from the sources of the Medway. I have drunk of the source of the Ribble also, but of no other small streams, for I pay them no honour. I drink of the greater rivers.

I have drunk of the sources of the Danube in the Black Forest during a piece of walking in connection with the campaign of Blenheim. I have drunk of the sources of the Rhone at its glacier—unpleasant water, and liable to give one goitre. And I have drunk from that solemn pool very high up in a lonely cup of the hills which is the true source of the Garonne. And I have drunk of the sources of the Moselle, but I had never yet drunk the water at the spring-head of the Seine, until the time of which I here write. I ought to have done this, for the Seine is the opposite number to the Thames, and of the spring of the Thames I did indeed most religiously drink in that year 1910 which was so wet a summer, or so wet at that moment, that the spring came out at the true Thameshead, in its meadow by the Fosse Way, where it had run dry for more than a lifetime. For when they made the canal (I think under George III, but anyhow a long time ago), joining the Thames Valley to the Severn, the first mile or so of the Thames dried up: which was a judgment on them. But in this year 1910, I say, it flowed again, at Thames Head in Thames Head Mead; and thereof I drank with full ritual, thereby acquiring jurisdiction over the whole valley from that place to Long Nose Buoy near the North Foreland, and entering into communion with all the territory of the stream and sharing sovereignty with it. At least, such is my imagination of the affair.

So the other day, as I was going to Burgundy, I thought I would at long last get similar virtue from the Seine, and having traced out carefully upon the map where the first water was likely to be found, I took a train to the nearest small railway station and set out towards the spot I had marked.

It was during broiling weather which beat down more fiercely upon those high Burgundian hills, I think, even than it did upon the glaring stones of Paris. Nevertheless, there was no way of getting to my goal except on foot, so I set out upwards, to cross the first watershed: there were two ridges between me and the head of the Seine valley.

I found, as one always does if one takes a journey with an individual motive, unusual, personal, and remote, delightful things upon my way. I found two villages as secluded as Templecombe used to be when I was a boy, and in the middle of one of them I found the house of a very wise man who was also reasonably rich. He was walking in his garden. We were separated only by great high gates of wrought iron which belonged to another age. I was so fatigued with my walk in that heat that I sat down on the stonework of his entrance and made an excuse to talk to him, asking him how far I was from the first stream of the river. He was pleased to think that a stranger was worshipping the Seine, and told me how often he had visited this same neighbouring place and how I should best get to it; but all the while he stayed behind his grating, so that I had to talk to him as one would talk to the lion at the Zoo. The reason I call him wise is, first that he did not ask me in, as he knew nothing about me; and secondly, that when he asked me how I liked his deep valley, and when I had praised it, he told me he had come there of set purpose, when petrol first became a menace, and had lived there ever since, and was now secure from the world. I could not sufficiently praise this spirit, although it prevented him from having a road near his house: there was only the cobbled way upon which I was going, and I suppose there had never been a proper highway to the place, but only these earth lanes and bridle paths, since it was built. And that must have been (as appeared from its style) in the end of the seventeenth century, when squires did all their travel on horseback.

So I went on up from this chance wise man into a wood upon the last ridge, and when I came out of this wood at the summit I found myself on a bare upland, which was part of the main watershed of Europe. To the south I could see over the tops of the trees of a great forest which fell away and away towards Dijon, and beyond to the Burgundian vineyards. Perhaps if it had been clearer I might have seen very faint against the horizon the grey line of the Bressian Hills, which are the bulwark of the Jura beyond the Clairvaux plain. But that summer weather, though it made the distances more profound, did not show things extremely distant as might have a threat of spring rain.

To the north the land seemed to fall away eternally in a slow shelf indented by those deep coombes wherein the utmost streams arise, and among them the Seine which I was seeking, into which they all fall at last. As I so looked northward, it seemed almost as though there were no end to the prospect, and as though all the mid-north to the capital itself were spread out under my gaze. That of course was imagination only, for Paris was nearly as far away as Chester is from London. Still, all the land did so fall away, without interruption, and from that roof and summit, I say, there seemed to be no end to it.

Then, leaving the prospect, I looked closer by to the glen at my feet, and taking out my map, I worked out where I should most likely find the first beginnings of that famous water, and to seek it I scrambled down through the rough thorn-studded pastures—therein I saw to my great pleasure the first trickle and runnel of a rill. I had feared that the great drought would have killed it, and that, coming at such a time, I should fail to see the true Head of Seine beginning its flow. But it seems that there are reserves of water in these hills, and that this hardly ever runs quite dry, though one could see by the width of gravel that in winter there must be a broader stream. I knelt down, therefore, immediately where the gravel first showed against the grass, and where a tiny thread of water could just be made out among the little stones. And of this I carefully drank, remembering as I did so all the other great rivers which had come into my possession, and praying that before I died I might do the same by the Elbe and the Vistula, which I have missed. Having done this, I sauntered some few miles down the valley and came to a small town surrounding a great abbey church called St. Seine. I have not read the history of it, so I do not know; but I imagine that in the far past someone had deified the river, and that this worship had descended in honest and Christian fashion to later times. At any rate, there it was, giving its maimed benediction (for the community was destroyed long since) to the beginnings of the Seine's prodigious pilgrimage.

Some day I shall follow it down till I come to the place where it will first float a boat, and then I shall drift along, carrying my boat at the weirs, until I come to the lower valley, and then I shall carry on to Rouen and to the sea; and after that I shall be able to say and boast that I really know the river. I say, "I shall do so." But shall I? I doubt it. For there are years in which one can plan for the future and fulfil; but there are other years, later on (and these are upon me), when the pleasant things of this world have to be enjoyed in the mind alone.

On Making an Omelette

I HAVE had the pleasure and the great honour of writing in my time upon the consoling theme that he writes best on any subject who knows least about it. Thus, I might write upon playing the violin, or the possible connection between the agglutinative languages of the Mongolian group (including the Magyar) and what I am told are the astonishing varieties of the American-Indian tongues both north and south.

But in the matter of omelettes I am in a more difficult position, for I can both make an omelette and yet not make it. I am of those who can create an omelette to delight the taste but not the eye. Therefore, according to whether you prefer the look of the food or the taste of it (in other words, August Reader, according to whether you are a fool or a glutton), I am one who can or who cannot make omelettes.

But that is neither here nor there. Omelettes are my theme (or rather the making of omelettes). To hymn omelettes (or rather the making of omelettes) do I strike the lyre.

It was said by a wise man whose name is lost in the night of time (nor does it matter to him or to us that his name should be lost—what is a posthumous name compared with a living soul?), it has been repeated by a hundred others, each of whom claims to be the originator, that "you cannot make an omelette without breaking eggs." By this epigram it was established that you can do nothing great or sudden in this world without injustice, baseness, violence, suffering, futility, and horror. On this account some will add: "Do nothing great or sudden." On this I will not delay. I will return to the making of omelettes.

The making of omelettes has about it a lesson to be discovered in all other things of man's creation. It was expressed by our grandmothers in the phrase, "There is a right and a wrong way of boiling an egg." But then, our grandmothers did not know how to make omelettes. There is nothing made by man, no, not even his false religions, which for full success requires so complete a conduct of the affair as the making of an omelette.

I had thought when I first considered this great subject, that the omelette being the perfection of cooking, it must also be, as it were, upon the apex of time; since it is admitted that we are the summits of the human race and far the superiors of all who have gone before us, it should therefore be acknowledged that in the supreme matter of all, which is eating (unless indeed you give drinking a certain priority between the twins), we have arrived at an acme. And since the perfect omelette is the perfection of all cooking, we are here upon the very peak.

Well then, if the omelette be the crown of Man's achievement, the most glorious of his acts and the full fruit of time (I mean the omelette as you may eat it now, not the despicable omelette of some few years ago in the court of the Regent or on St. Michael's Mount, or in the very large hotel at Sisteron which used to be kept by a hussar turned civilian)—if the omelette, I say, be the supreme achievement of Man and his principal title to have something divine about him, and the best witness to his supernal origin, it behoves us to understand very thoroughly the making of an omelette.

But wait a moment. Let us first consider the egg and talk to it kindly, for, in the making of an omelette, more than one egg will be sacrificed. Indeed, it is a just rule that according to the number that are to eat the omelette, double that number of eggs should be sacrificed—unless indeed you have a very great number at table, such as a dozen, and one or two of them be poor relations, who will naturally be served last. In such cases you can dock an egg or two; but, roughly speaking, two eggs to the man or the woman is the Omelette Canon.

Before we sacrifice the egg we owe it that reverence which is due to victims. We may tell it that it might have been an innocent good egg (and the Good Egg is the symbol of all good things) and have achieved its rightful British end: boiled, poached or even scrambled. But it is called to a higher destiny; it is to be merged in the great unity; it is to lose its foolish desire for any personal eggish immortality or particular glory of egg-in-the-shell. It is to be resolved into the Omelette τὸ πᾶν. Let him be told that, in some way he does not understand (nor I either, for that matter), such a fate is better than carrying on.

That done, let us proceed to break him (for, alas! he

must be broken, since all things temporal are broken), and begin making our omelette.

But wait one moment. There is something else to be considered. Omelettes are of various kinds. What sort of omelette would you make? It depends upon your company, upon your taste, upon tradition, upon convention, upon opportunity. If I had the time I would establish a full category of all the various gates by which omelette-making can be entered; of all the various final causes for which the omelette is set upon its course.

There is the omelette of the Campo Romano—that plain in summer blazing, in winter frozen; that sterile stony land (yet productive of a strong wine) which lies between the trickle of the Ebro and the parched sources of the Upper Tagus. *There* flourishes the Tortilla; an Omelette with bits of potato in it, quite stiff, so that you may slap it like the sole of a slipper. Then there is the rough Peasant Omelette, with lumps of bacon thrown in, jumbled in anyhow, jumped upon a wooden fire, very succulent. There is your Hotel Omelette, which is kept (from the reverence they bear you) for half an hour or so hardening upon a sort of grating above the stove. In such an omelette there is no salt, and it kills. There are little derivative Second Cousin Omelettes, such as your Jam Omelette, your Rum Omelette, your Flaming Omelette, your Tomato Omelette, your Horrible Gravy Omelette, your Excellent Cheese Omelette— which should not be made with Parmesan, by the way, but with old and dry Gruyère. There is your omelette which has no name, and to which now I return, because a strong memory in my mind compels me to do so.

It is—oh! my companions of so long ago!—that omelette made in a very large frying-pan borrowed or stolen from the nearest farm, in which pan young men fry equally borrowed or stolen butter, breaking into it eggs equally borrowed or stolen, digging out the salt from their haversacks, picking up onions from the fields. They eat it together all out of the pan, in wolfish fashion, and are the better for the deed. Best is that omelette of travel or of manœuvres, of the mountains or of the wide, open, lonely fields, when it is made at night and when the crackling fire (of stolen wood) startles the darkness and lights from below the faces of the eager boys and shines in their eyes. Such an omelette may properly be called the O.P., or Omelette of Paradise.

Now that I have written so far, you may ask me, "How then should the true Domestic Omelette be made?" You will say to me, "I have often wondered how it should be done. I have often tried to make it. I have always failed. What are the rules? Into this dark life wherein we go groping all the time, come, rise like an orient-star before the morning and lead us down the radiant way."

Very well. I consent. I will now tell you, my children, how to make a perfect omelette. First take some eggs. Then beat them up. Put in what you think will taste nice (and salt is an advantage). Fry it over a fire. Your omelette will appear. It will either be good or bad. I will lay three hundred pounds to a piece of any modern European Government stock at a hundred years' purchase that it will be not good but bad. Never mind. All our efforts in this world are of this disappointing kind. It is so with our characters and with our investments, and with our horrible books, and even with our attempts at serving our fellow-men—our sincere attempts at serving them.

Be content to remember that those who can make omelettes properly can do nothing else. And thank the Lord that you have other talents.

★ V ★

The Place of Recovery

I KNOW a man who is what people to-day call a mystic. It is a wrong use of the term, but no matter; if I were to use the word in its right sense it would not apply, and in this wrong sense everyone will understand it.

He came to me the other day to drink a glass of wine after dinner, and when we had talked upon different things for a little while he suddenly proposed this:

"Do you think anything is ever lost?"

"Why, yes," said I. "I should have thought everything was lost sooner or later and most things pretty quickly."

He answered: "When you have risen out of yourself into something more, say, under the influence of music; then when the influence ceases, when the experience becomes a memory, fades—do you think it is therefore done with, and for ever?"

"I suppose so," said I. "Unless one can get an opportunity of hearing the *morceau* again."

He tossed his head impatiently: "And the great loves? And the landscapes? And the fresh keenness of new things in youth? And the fixed resolves?" he cried.

To this list of his I added, for my own part: "And

the Chambertin of the 'Three Pheasants.' And the Richebourg which they gave me the time after."

He bore with the interruption, and then, leaning forward, with his hands between his knees and gazing at the fire, he said: "Listen to this. The other day I had what you may call a dream. But I am not too sure that it was a dream. There are times in which I feel that what we call waking is only half-living and that the visions alone are true. This was my vision, real, as I still believe, though it came to me in the night when my soul was apart from my body.

"I discovered myself to be in a place of which something told me from within that it had a sacred name, and was called 'The Place of Recovery.' There was no defined landscape about it, nor any certain environment. It might have been an ancient Great House or a garden —the sensation was of both combined, and all about it was an air of achieved and well-filled repose. Though no external environment affected me, I was very vividly conscious of human spirits who were there met, and (even as they spoke) of certain material things: or, at any rate, the experience of certain material things. So that when my companions spoke of these I saw them before me, the things of which they spoke, and could have touched them, as we can see and touch things in dreams —or rather in visions.

"But at first they said nothing of things, but only of happenings, and among their earliest words I heard from one of them, and the most beloved, out of the past, a chance allusion to one small incident which for many years had tortured me with remorse. In that one allusion I stood bewildered, and I openly confessed: 'Surely,'

25

said I, 'you have forgotten! I answered you bitterly and foolishly' (I quoted my very words), 'and the memory of that wound inflicted in a moment, in an accident—oh! not of my will—has wounded me in turn: wounded me to death.' But that which was speaking to me answered with complete simplicity: 'I do not understand what you are saying. You must have had an evil dream. You never said such words! Never, never did you speak unkindly to me.' And this answer was true, so that my memory in the matter, if memory it were, ceased to be, and the pristine glory was restored.

"Then others crowded about me, great also, though lesser than that first consoler; and the one, the next, the third, each made it clear that sins and weaknesses and misunderstandings and certain abominations had never been. Then came another troupe who spoke lesser, indeed, but still amazing words: how what I had suffered, not of my own action, but in sympathy with them, was undone, or rather had not been. How this one had not been pierced through the heart with a sword, nor that one dishonoured, nor the other despised of the world: how the young gaiety whose decline I thought I had witnessed had never sunk with the years into despair.

"Then there passed before me in majestic and divine procession a lovely landscape desecrated (as I had once thought) by Avarice and War, and lovely buildings ruined and pulled down, and lovely ornaments destroyed. How many there were I know not, but in mighty numbers (yet not confused) one after another rose before my sight, domestic or majestic, small things and great. Every one of them, town, field and wood, palace and shrine and marble, was there complete and re-established. Do you know, will you believe, that I wandered, not by memory but in actual life through the old Hampstead of 1880 and that I saw the Roman Champaign through the gate of St. John Lateran as once it showed when I was young? I saw the view in all its old expanse, unbarred by monstrous modern walls. Also did I find my own home of another day.

"In all this there was no regret, and (what most convinces me of the reality of the affair) there was no fear nor expectation of change.

"It pains me to descend to lesser things, but you must hear the whole truth. Messengers conveyed it to me that the moneys I had foolishly spent had been well spent indeed. I discovered their results and was the richer thereby. Money squandered, turned into money invested; and material objects, which I had valued rather for their price than from affection, took on their form again.

"You see how I am sparing you nothing, but telling you the whole truth, and how in the Place of Recovery the whole of man is satisfied, even in the base little business of getting and spending." He sighed, and paused.

"Tell me," said I, interrupting him for the first time, "was the care-free heart recovered in that place? Did you find yourself without responsibility again—like all animals, most children, and some few happy men? And did they lead to you by the hand that charming girl known as Our Innocence?"

But he went on, ignoring me: "I will tell you one thing last, because it is the most trivial. There was brought to me with deference a certain receptacle of rare

27

wood inlaid, and moving noiselessly upon magic wheels, wherein were heaped up all the coins and bank-notes I had ever dropped or mislaid. There was a whole little hill of sixpences and threepenny and fourpenny bits; a big foundation of pennies; green and pink and white crinkly paper and two cheques (each of which I vividly recognised because those who drew them had refused to draw them again after I had lost them), and, gleaming in the mass, were not a few of the old-fashioned golden sovereigns and half-sovereigns . . ."

At this moment the telephone which is in my room rang, but when I went to it an unknown voice asked not for me but for my friend.

"It is you that are wanted," I said, "though I don't know how they knew you were here."

"Oh," answered the Mystic, rising hurriedly, "I told someone where to ring me up this evening in case it was necessary. I hope you don't mind?"

Then he settled himself solidly on a chair with an intent look on his face as of the things that really matter. "Yes? . . . No!" (His face became grave.) "It can't be! . . . New York is only five hours earlier than London. 'Change is shut. . . . Oh, Chicago. . . ." There was a pause of about thirty seconds during which the nasty little instrument went on making a squeaking noise, and as it gave him the news his face went dead white and his mouth drew into a violent shape. "*Twenty-nine?* It Can't Be! You mean thirty-nine! . . ." A shorter pause. He became agitated. He moved his free hand up and down irresponsibly and he shouted at the wretched scientific contraption: "But they were forty-one only yesterday. . . . You can't help it? . . . Of course you can't help it!"

He jammed the receiver back and staggered to his feet. He looked at me dully for a moment, then he dived for the door.

"I must see what can be done," he muttered. I tried to help him on with his coat, but he snatched it from me, and was off at a run into the road.

★ VI ★

Old Brisach

THE extent to which places famous in the history of war lose their importance and their effect upon the mind of contemporaries varies along a scale which reaches from complete forgetfulness to active contemporary use. At one end of such a scale, for instance, you have Portsmouth, Verdun, the Brenner—places filled with arms for centuries and to this day; at the other, the zero end, or nearly approaching to zero, the forgotten places, I should specially quote as an example Old Brisach.

It is a fair guess that out of a hundred men well instructed in the general history of Europe, perhaps one may be familiar with the name; and even those who have read military history considerably have for the most part forgotten that point which, in a critical moment of Europe, was the centre of observation—a point upon the fate of which depended all our future. Old Brisach, then, is of the forgotten things: the arch-forgotten. It is so forgotten that it knows itself to be forgotten. It even asks the few who visit it at all to visit it in connection with sundry old stories of the Middle Ages which have nothing to do with its brief moment of glory and disaster and its playing of a high human part; and I

30

know of at least two guide-books which give its name and tell you nothing of what it was as a fortress.

In the years just before the outbreak of the Great Rebellion in England, at the opening of the second third of the seventeenth century, the last effort was being made and war almost universal waged to determine this issue: whether Christendom should be reunited in religion and therefore in culture, or whether nationalism and a profound division between the culture of the north and the south should be the chief marks of her future. Upon the one side of this prodigious struggle stood the Hapsburg cousins, who governed the Empire, Spain and the New World. On the other stood the French Monarchy, that fraction of the Netherlands which had successfully rebelled against the Spanish King, and the Protestant Princes of Germany. The latter conquered, for they were successful in frustrating the efforts of the former. They did not conquer in the sense that they won the decisive battle of a definite campaign or positively imposed their wills upon their opponents; but their resistance was effective, and well before the end of the struggle in 1648 it was clear that the future would lie with nationalism and with a divided Europe.

For the success of the Hapsburg effort it was essential that the then overwhelming military power of Spain should be constantly in touch with the Empire and able to reach the revolted provinces in the Netherlands. For this double task it had two avenues of approach: 1, certain passes in the Alps, 2, the narrow way west of the hills which gets water-carriage by the Rhine valley. Now along this last, which may be regarded as a chain the breaking of any link in which would break the whole,

Brisach was the main strong point. It stood on its fine, steep, isolated rock above the Rhine, overlooking beyond the stream the Alsatian plain towards Colmar and the Vosges, with the country of the Black Forest behind it. Bernard of Saxe-Weimar besieged it with no very large forces, certainly less than twenty thousand men, and probably in useful effectives not much more than twelve thousand; and it fell. He was in the pay of the French, but he had been promised as his reward to be made a sort of sovereign over a German Alsace. He died in the midst of his triumph, while all Nothern Europe and France were reeling with the news that the enemy's main artery had been cut. A French officer in his service, surviving him, persuaded the victorious force to hand over the fruits of their victory to the French King—and upon that fall of Brisach, the capture of that embattlemented rock above the Rhine, was founded the French hold on Alsace, with all that has come of it—the independence of Holland, the general success of the opposition to the Hapsburgs, the failure of the Austrian and Spanish effort.

If history were a living thing to men, or were taught as it should be in our schools, the Rock of Brisach would mean a great deal more than the Rock of Gibraltar. I should blush to say that I was the only modern man who ever visited it for the sake of the siege—I am sure that would be nonsense; but at any rate I found it quite deserted, and no one in Freiburg or in Colmar, its two neighbours, aware of any pilgrimage to the place, however rare. To visit it and stand upon its platform (it is a tiny town, hardly more than a fort) was like going to an empty tomb, rifled of treasure. I heard that tourists would come and see the big church, but nothing more. I looked down over those small man-made precipices of wall and had below me the ground which had decided our fate; but I have never come across anyone who had travelled to experience that emotion. The little shallow Rhine goes rapidly by, crossed by a crazy bridge of boats; and in the air all about is silence. So much for Old Brisach. I should like to put it under glass.

There is another thing in connection with that ought-to-be immortal name: the contrast between Old Brisach and New. The better part of a lifetime after the fall of the fortress Louis XIV had to restore it to Austria. But he was determined not to restore the key-value which Old Brisach had held. So on the opposite bank, to command the crossing, he made of one piece, artificially, New Brisach. And nowhere in Europe will you see the contrast between the last warfare of the old days and the warfare of the new more vivid. Old Brisach on its clean, stubborn, precipitous rock, had been, since the Roman legions first came there, dependent upon the aboriginal principle of a stronghold: that it should be a place dominating the attack, difficult to assault from below, steep, giving every advantage to the possessor of the crown thereof against men on foot who would attempt to swarm up its sides. New Brisach is on the dead flat plain, and is strong through earth, trench and rampart and the star-work which the genius of Vauban both summarised and founded. The plan of it might be quoted as a perfect paradigm, a little model, of what the fortress of the precise and regular warfare which opens with the campaigns of Louis XIV and ends with the Great War should be. It is especially a model of those enclosed works which everywhere bear testimony to the sieges that run from the 'sixties of the seventeenth century to the Crimea. Whether it has itself ever stood a regular siege I do not know; but it was designed for the most prolonged resistance; and that immense husk of earthwork and wall and moat surrounding the small kernel of the exact little regular town within—just sufficient to harbour its garrison and no more—is still a marvel perfectly preserved. It would have delighted the eye of Sterne's Corporal, and would have spurred to eagerness in its capture the eye of John Churchill, who tackled its predecessor at Bouchain.

To visit New Brisach, and then Old Brisach after it, is to visit two museum specimens taken out of two eras, and yet one man could have lived from presence in youth at the siege of Old Brisach to hearing in old age of New Brisach's completion. To visit the two to-day is like peering, in some collection of armament, first at an arquebus, then at a rifle. And both are dead. Both are fossils. As fossils I hope they will be retained. Profoundly do I hope that the iconoclastic French will not in a fit of progress level the sombre tracery of Vauban's masterpiece. As profoundly do I hope, and with more security, that the reverent Germans will not touch a stone of the walls which surrendered to Bernard. There they stand, looking at each other, twins, forgotten, emblems, proud (I suppose), silent. Go some day and look at them. It is worth while.

In Honour of the Unicorn

THEY have found the Unicorn at last! Very glad I am that they have found him: glad for a number of reasons. They have found him in China, and high time too. They have found him not alive, but dead, and turned to a skeleton. They were too late, as usual. Had they taken a little trouble while he was still alive, they would have spotted him along ago and spared us a lot of non-sensical scepticism about fabulous monsters. Anyhow, he's safe home at last, and I welcome him.

Why should there not indeed be a unicorn any less than a Great Sea Serpent? And that the Great Sea Serpent lives and thrives no one who has read the evidence can doubt. Had they gone out a-hunting, they might have come on a unicorn any day of the week; there is always a fine one to be found nearby the house of any honest man, for they seek such company; and there are whole herds of them in Utopia. But they would not start in time, or look closely enough. It is just like them.

Some hundreds of years ago men from Arabia saw the unicorn with their own eyes and left a record of it. They saw it on the slopes of the Himalayas, and it answered to the name of Karkandan. They wrote a careful description of it. They were believed in their time. They have not been believed in ours, but time has done them justice and the skeleton of the unicorn has been found.

I say I am glad for many reasons. One is that perhaps we shall now be allowed to talk of the beast freely and without fear. As long as it was thought fabulous and was in the Royal Arms, no one could talk of it slightingly. Worship of the State having replaced older religions and falsehood having been deified as well, a thing at once believed to be false and accepted as an emblem of the State was above criticism. But now that the unicorn has turned out to be a real beast, like the donkey or the essay writer, he is fair game. Not that I want to say anything against him, but that I like to feel free.

He came into the Royal Arms (as a supporter) through the Stuarts; he was James I's beast; he is Scotch, or Scots, or Scottish. Before him the Dexter Supporter (if that is right—for I am no Herald) was I know not what: in Henry VIII's time it was a great dog. But James brought in the unicorn as I say: a Caledonian hippoid. He was therefore unpopular for about a hundred and fifty years. His colleague the lion had a very different fate. He stands for all that men most admire in themselves, such as ferocity, a good voice and a theatrical manner, so that he has been adopted by the majority with enthusiasm. The unicorn has more delicately stood in the background, and for this he should be honoured.

Now that he has been discovered, the time has come to test the horns of unicorns, which are to be found all up and down the world. In my voluminous reading upon this department of knowledge, I have found that all modern writers since, say, the French encyclopædists, affirm that these horns are the horns of a fish, and of a fish well known to have a long twisted horn and sometimes even two. I think it is called the narwhal: but then, is the narwhal a fish? Anyhow whether it be a fish or a fowl, unicorn's horns are said to be his and not of the unicorn at all. I mistrust these positive statements, especially when they are used to sneer at what the sneerer believes to be a myth. The process of his thought is clear enough. He is convinced (without proof and even without probability) that there was never such a thing as a unicorn. He is presented with a horn said to belong to a unicorn. By his creed he is not allowed to believe it to have belonged to a unicorn, so he looks out for the next most likely thing and calls it the horn of a narwhal. We all know this process of thought and, I hope, we have all learnt to despise it.

Now, as I muse upon the qualities of the unicorn, and in my joy at its discovery, I remember a whole list of other things which are long overdue for rehabilitation. For instance, there is the famous passage in Josephus which has been called an interpolation, but which now has been reinforced (so the scholars tell me) by the discovery of what is called the Russian Josephus.

There is also the still more famous letter to Agbar. I have always believed in that letter; for the simple reason that there is no reason why it should not have been written, and that no one doubted it till hundreds of years after it had disappeared. Even if there had been something marvellous about it, all history swarms with the marvellous or unusual; and even in our little lives we each of us have an example or two to show. But there was nothing marvellous about it. It was plain and straightforward. I suppose one of these days they will find that letter to Agbar and be able to test it. It was taken away by the Mohammedans and may well be preserved somewhere. Anyway, Eusebius believed in it, and he certainly knew more about those things than anyone of our time.

So with the unicorn. Aristotle believed in it, and Pliny believed in it. Pliny was very detailed about it—a little too detailed. I am not sure that Pliny's wealth of detail did not do something to discredit the poor monocerous ungulate. As for the unicorn of the Bible, it is a fraud. You must not jump to the conclusion that I am blaspheming Holy Writ, but I am assured by the only book in this room where I write (and I can't be bothered to fetch another) that "unicorn" in the Bible is only a mistranslation for something with at least two horns or perhaps three, but not one. It is a pity, for it takes away one of the great pro-unicorn arguments which would have appealed to the fundamentalists; but after all, now that we have the actual skeleton of the beast (and in China, too, where all the new startling relics come from), we need not depend upon the fundamentalist, or even upon the ancients. In this matter of the unicorn, we no longer live by faith but by reason, and that is always a great comfort.

Which reminds me, by way of an end, that the discovery of the unicorn is a most excellent example of how and why men in the mass believe or disbelieve a thing, to wit, because most other people around them believe or disbelieve it: so rational is man!

Of a thousand things on which a highly educated man is fully certain, there is perhaps one on which he has read the evidence thoroughly and understood it; the rest he takes from the air about him. The attitude of men towards their fellows who disbelieve a thing commonly accepted (such as astrology in the mid-seventeenth century, or to-day the little electron) is of exactly the same sort as that towards a person who wears a hat out of the fashion. If it became the fashion to balance a tiny top-hat on the top of one's head and keep it brushed the wrong way, a man who turned up at a wedding with a glossy top-hat which fitted him would be an outcast. So a man incredulous of the fashionable theory of his time is an outcast. Most men would deny that foundation to their faith, but if you were to put them through the Socratean mill and ask them searching questions they would betray themselves. They would use such phrases as "Why, everybody knows . . . !" or "He is the only person to say . . .", and by the time that you had turned them inside out you would find that their mood was what I have called it: fashion and nothing more.

One age is not more credulous than another, only it is credulous about a different sort of thing. Those who are both well informed and lively in temperament are apt to be most disgusted with the follies of their own time. But I am not sure that the follies of our day, especially its enormous credulities, are much worse than those of our fathers. Anyhow, the credulities will go on, and if we lose one lot we shall catch another, as surely as a man in losing his gullibility catches avarice, and in losing avarice (if that be possible) catches poverty and all the contempt accompanying same.

One steadfast thing remains, and that is the permanent comedy of watching the change. So for my part I do hope to live until that perhaps immediate day when the fantastic figures of astronomy will burst and the stars will be at reasonable distances again: as they are even now to a friend of mine, who estimates the sun at twelve miles, the moon at twenty, and all the stars at a common distance (about a hundred miles) from the earth; and, firm in this faith, is as happy as one can be in this world.

★ VIII ★

On Fitting Things In

SOME weeks ago I read a poem by Mr. Galsworthy called *Never Get Out*. It was about a cat in a cage. Having read it, I sat down at once and wrote another poem on the same lines about a man. It was all about a man who didn't pull things off; who wasn't a success; one of those men who go about in the neighbourhood of their sixtieth year with pale, weak eyes and sunken corners to their lips. My poem was called *Never Get On*. It ended with very noble lines which, for the love I bear you, and because you have never previously heard them, I will now proceed to recite:

> He died in despair, and in debt, and a ditch,
> The poor old Incompetent Son of a Bitch,
> Never Get On!

It was a very sad poem. I ought not to have written it, for it was not a moral poem. It implied that the fruit of men's actions does not depend upon their will, but upon something over which they have no control. However, who can resist the Muse, whithersoever she tends? When I had completed this lyric (of which I have given you but the bare conclusion) I pondered seriously for

41

some moments upon the invitation to despair which it contained. I blamed my Muse, and would have dealt with her drastically had she not prudently vanished, not to appear again (if I know anything of her) till September next at the earliest. I had been led into a false philosophy, and I could not help dwelling upon the truths whereon that false philosophy is based. They are not comforting truths. The most prominent of them has been expressed by the popular wisdom of mankind in many proverbs, discoverable in all languages. The English one is this:

"One man may steal a horse where another mayn't look over the hedge." Another remotely connected with it, but connected all the same, is "Kissing goes by favour." And the whole may be summed up in the bitter judgment of some millions who have tried the temper of mankind: "There is no justice in this world."

When I was young it puzzled me not a little that one man could steal a horse where another man might not look over the hedge. On the one hand, I had discovered that this was true; on the other hand, I knew as well as I knew the first principles of reasoning in geometry (now discredited but in my youth tenable enough) that Justice was eternal. I knew that if you butt your head against the eternal you break it; Justice, therefore, should prevail; yet here were people suffering intolerable things for looking over hedges while dozens of horse-stealers were having the time of their lives.

It was not till lately that the revelation came to me which solved this mystery. It was the observation of this third thing—that in matters of the moment (not in eternal things) all depends on Fitting In. If you Fit In, well and good; if you don't, hell and misery. It is true primarily of stoppers of bottles, but in a lesser degree of getting a seat in the Tube, of passing a pleasant evening at dinner, indeed of not noticing your clothes; and it is especially true of selling books or getting an audience for what you write.

Now here, since all men are most at their ease when they talk shop, I will talk shop. Only, before doing so, let me exemplify that truth.

I say all men are best at their ease when they are talking shop. It is because they then have most material to hand, and because they are dealing with the thing which, if they will confess it, most occupies their minds. Indeed, men apologise for talking shop precisely because their inclination to do so is so strong. It may bore those who are not of the trade, but on this page, by your leave, we are all of the trade. Except for a little of the stuff called politics, we discuss nothing but how men write, why they write, when they write, if they write, whether they should write, and (when we have done with all that) when, how, if, and whether they write about the writings of others. Oh, fruitful and creative trade! Oh, Scribbling, glory of the State! Oh, strengthening of England! Oh, best proof of civic freedom and of our active participation in the great business of being governed by consent!

Well then, to talk shop in this connection, the great principle of Fitting In most assuredly governs the getting of an audience for written things. No one can tell you wherein the fitness lies, but the truth remains that in the fitness the result resides.

If you doubt this, I will provide you with a simple

experiment which will test the matter thoroughly. Go to a public library and borrow *Paradise Lost*. Copy out in your own handwriting some twenty lines describing any one of the glorious landscapes in the fourth book of that masterpiece. Sign it with your name, entitle it "Lines on a fair prospect," and send it to any editor you like. Accompany it with a letter saying that as it has so often been rejected you will be obliged to get it back in the enclosed stamped envelope. It will come back to you like a boomerang.

Similarly, there was an experienced and soured man of the world who said, on making a peroration to a public meeting (while the audience was fighting to get out of the only door), "You might as well read Theocritus to a cow."

By all this I do not mean anything so silly as that the Many cannot judge what is good. In the long run it is the Many who establish what is good. What I mean is that if you Fit In you Fit In, and if you don't you don't. Make up your mind to it, and you will fulfil the great saying of Bismarck: "Blessed are they that expect nothing, for they shall not be disappointed." Imagine a French politician addressing an English audience, or a Welsh politician addressing a French one, or a Chinese mandarin persuading to order a mob of youths coming out of a football match; or Bellarmine or Suarez publishing a treatise for a London daily paper. Imagine what would be their fate. And why would they suffer it? Because they did not Fit In.

There are men who desire consolation for the accidents of this world. If they seek it in eternity they are to be praised; if they seek it in their own moment they are to be despised as fools. The world is indefinitely complicated, its combinations change with every moment. No one exactly Fits In except just with one place and time; no one even roughly Fits In except in his own place and time, as he and they happen to fall during the perpetual eddy and flux.

Are we, then, to attempt, by some forcing of ourselves, to Fit In? God forbid! Least of all should we writing men attempt it. Unlike the singer who can at least notice when people are talking to themselves out loud, and, still better, can notice the individuals who get up and go out in the middle of his song; unlike the actor who to-day, in spite of the police, is occasionally hissed; unlike his little brother the politician, who is free to hear the song "Sit down—sit down" sung to the tune of Big Ben chimes, or the first verse of "Tell me the old, old story"—unlike all these, I say, we writers are not in touch with our audience. All we know is that we write a book and it is pulped; then twenty years later it is reissued and makes a fortune. Why that is so the publisher doesn't know, the publisher's reader doesn't know, certainly the critic doesn't know. Nobody knows. It isn't chance, it's Fitting In.

Make an effort to Fit In, and you will most abominably fail. Go ahead simply, do what lies before you, and you will probably fail also. Do nothing, and you will quite certainly fail; in fact, that is the only certitude there is in the whole unpleasant business.

There are some men who Fit In with the world at large, a much bigger affair than the petty trade of writing. At any rate, they Fit In with their own particular province, and they are the blessed of this world.

They owe their fortune to no effort of their own. They may be told by their seamless faces, contented eyes, and general fatuity. There are others at the further end of the scale who don't Fit In at all. They may be told by the torture on their brows and the unsatisfied longing of their gaze. Of these, some few are the fathers of a new world, but the most part are misfits in between, and hence the general disgruntlement of mankind, the perpetual looking for more and more advanced politics and in a word, the endless grinding of an empty mill.

If any of these words of mine have left you less foolishly contented than you were, I shall not have laboured in vain.

★ IX ★

Autobiography

ONE might ask oneself two questions about autobiography: Why are there so few autobiographies? Why are so few autobiographies tolerable?

The answer to the first question is easier than the answer to the second. I think we all know why there are so few autobiographies. Most of us have been in the mood to write them, and none, or hardly any of us, have written them. So we know. How many of those who read these lines can honestly say that they have never been in the mood to write their lives? I'm sure I have! And how many can so much as say that they have begun the task? I'm sure I haven't. Now we all of us know the reason. And, take it full and bye, it is one of the very few things to be honoured in our nature. It is *Pudor*, a word for which, thanks to the completely modern quality of modern English, there is no modern equivalent. It is that element of salvation in us which prevents us from singing at the top of our voices in railway carriages—at least, when there are strangers condemned to the same box. Much as I regret to record one single point in favour of the Fallen Race of Eoanthropos,

47

that is the fact. We preserve a little shrine; we keep a little hedged field. We are (for once) to be commended.

That we should desire to write our lives is inevitable. They are much the most interesting tragedy we know; much the fullest in detail; much the most absorbing. We are not withheld (God knows!) by diffidence—which is a very different thing from *Pudor*: as different as milk from brandy—nor are we restrained only by laziness, though I will honourably grant something in the result to that excellent ingredient; no, we are restrained at heart by *this* feeling: "Why should I cast these pearls before my snouted fellow-citizens? Why should I open the Holy of Holies?"

There is in this restraint a touch of immortality, I think. There is in it the positive sense of immortality, which is in contrast with the mere wistfulness for it. If, being wistful for immortality, we desire to write down all those dear details of how we stood for the Indian Civil in 1894 and were run into Bow Street on the night of the Boat Race, yet a consciousness within us that such great things live on to the eternal spheres allows us to disdain the necessity of putting them upon paper.

But a fig for all the reasons, and to Huddersfield with all this analysis of motive! The fact is there. We want to write autobiography and we don't; at least, I don't, and I hope you don't.

But now to that second and more difficult question. Of the autobiographies written, why are so few worth reading?

You may tell me that ninety-seven out of a hundred of the novels now written are little more than very putrid autobiography. I agree. But that does not answer the question; for of all novels now written, how many are worth reading? Of autobiographies frankly intended to be so, called so on the title page, and beginning with such words as "I very well remember the old house at Buffington—" or "My father's family came from Norfolk, but my mother's was connected with the Lyles of Clapham"—how many are tolerable? I can recall—and it is one of the very few forms of literature that the jaded read with ease—perhaps half a dozen. But when they are good it may be said of them, as of omelettes, that they are excellent. For just as there is nothing between the admirable omelette and the intolerable, so with autobiography; and the same applies to the laughter of women, to street singers, to acting, to professions of affection and to vinegar. (I am here sorely tempted to digress on vinegar, well knowing that for most people vinegar is but a sour taste; but if you had been where I have been, and had savoured what I have savoured, you would know that there is that vinegar which is of Paradise, and all the rest is not even wine gone bad, but mere chemicals. I resume.)

We may take it that what makes a good autobiography is undiscoverable, nor subject to analysis; and that saves a lot of trouble. No one can tell you what makes good verse, no one can tell you what makes the glad eye; no one can tell you what makes the thrill of a contralto voice; in the same way no one can tell you what makes a good autobiography. But since there is such a thing as the good autobiography, let us thank God for it and pass along. We find therein, as in first love, and in second, third and fourth and fifth love, something of ourselves and something of another. We find adventure, we enjoy discovery, we also mix domestically with a home. But what I suppose is best about a good autobiography is the way in which we carry along.

I knew a man once who told me that the thing he had most enjoyed in his life was drifting down a full river in an unknown land, gently touching the waters with the paddle of his canoe, sleeping on the wholesome bank at evening and carrying on from open day to open day. He was fortunate enough to have found unknown land, and a full river, and conditions without peril and solitude all combined. Now, good autobiographies are of this kind.

I suppose the writers of them, the half-dozen writers of them, combine a good deal of vanity with a good deal of luck in their lives, and a very great deal of vivid perception, a strong memory, an indifference to the more profound emotions. But really I don't know. They may supplement a bad memory with imagination; they may be telling atrocious lies all the time; they may have emotions as profound as the Great Mammoth Cave of Kentucky and prefer to conceal them. The point is the *result*; they are readable. An immense self-satisfaction— something much viler than vanity—is no bad quality in your autobiographer; it was the saving of old Gibbon.

And here let me say that I do not count the various Confessions. I do not call them autobiography. They are no more autobiography than melodrama turning on an historical character is history. Nor do I count the Diarists, who are not telling us about themselves but about Days and Works, and about those tiresome people called The Others.

Still less do I count the writers who give us a particular chronicle of the part they played in great affairs. Their books are commonly called Memoirs after the French. They are often interesting in parts, more commonly dull; they are never interesting throughout. They are hardly ever quite dull throughout, but their appeal lies in something outside the life of the writer. With autobiography the whole pleasure—if it is well done—lies in the following of one connected chain of inward personal experience.

Why have no true autobiographies survived from a remote antiquity? (Perhaps I ought to except the description of his life by that Indian conqueror, that Mongol Mohammedan, whose name I have forgotten, but to whose excellent writing I can testify through a translation which I have upstairs at this very moment and know exactly where to find, but will not be at the pains to seek.) Why have we no great classical autobiographies? (If we have, I apologise.) I take it to lie in this: that autobiography demands a common medium between the writer and the reader, more than does any other form of letters. That is why, I suppose, autobiography in one language does not commonly go down with the readers of another.

Autobiography is not easily translatable. What soldier returning from the ruins of Napoleon's army after the retreat from Moscow would have lingered lovingly upon *Reminiscences of a Buckinghamshire Parsonage*, excellent though it be? Or what Englishman worthy of public school tradition and duly moved by *All Quiet on the Western Front* or *Moans of a Scandinavian* could tolerate *Ma Pièce?* Or what dealer in oriental carpets upon the littoral of the Mediterranean, itinerant, impecunious, could forget himself for hours in Miss Bilberry's description of her Ohio home—though I will not deny that Miss Bilberry might read with avidity the autobiography of the itinerant seller of oriental carpets (and cocaine) were he not too wise to undertake the drudgery of writing such a book; but her reasons would not be truly autobiographical, and she is therefore no test.

To all this need of sympathy there is one exception; men will always read good autobiographies of animals. But then they are not written by animals; and I swear that no animal ever yet read an autobiography written by a man. This solemn truth may offend the fond lover of beasts, but truth it is. Meditate upon it.

X

Two Kings

I DO not remember to have seen, anywhere, a contrast or a parallel between Louis XIII, King of France, and his nephew, Charles II, King of England. Indeed, the singular opportunity for such parallel and contrast never occurred to me until the other day, when, fresh from the recent study of a portrait of Louis, I happened upon the engraving of another portrait, that of Charles at nearly the same period of his life; and immediately the very striking physical resemblance and, if expression be a guide, moral resemblance between the two struck me with the greatest force.

I do not know where that strange cast of face came into the Stuart and Bourbon blood: features long, almost concave, heavy-lipped, dark-haired, and—what is much the most striking point and the least easy to describe—a sort of slow, half-veiled look in the eyes. You have it in four faces at least, all related, and similar although moulded externally by such very different fortunes. You have it in Louis XIII; you have it in Charles; you have it in Louis XIV, and you have it in Monmouth.

For years I had stood in doubt whether Monmouth were really Charles's son or no. His mother was such a trull, and he was fathered upon Charles when that prince was so young, that there is plenty of substance for the strong belief of contemporaries that he was of another parentage. But the portrait painted after death (the severed head in the National Portrait Gallery) convinces me. I had heard men say that it was clearly Stuart, but the term was wrong. There was nothing of James I in it, or of Mary or of Darnley. There was very strongly marked upon it that new character which I have described, that character which comes in with the seventeenth century, has not appeared before, does not appear later—for the Pretenders show little sign of it. Seeing that, I could not doubt the relation between Monmouth and the King.

It must have come in some way through the Médicis, though, there again, you certainly don't find it in the Queen Mother, Marie de Médicis. She was a big, heavy, aggresive woman, with a large, coarse but not undignified face, fond of active rule and incapable of it. There was nothing in her (that one can trace) of that singular restraint and expression. From whatever blood it came, it stamped itself almost violently upon three generations—and then it disappeared.

The similarity between the uncle and the nephew, Louis XIII of France and Charles II of England, was not only one of face and expression, it was also one of figure; and I fancy, if one had seen them walking, one would have found a similarity of gait. What we cannot test, and what would be most instructive of all, must have been the living voice; and there also I fancy you would have found similarity. There is similarity also in the type of tenacity in each. It was a secretive tenacity: openly secretive, if I may so express myself, in Louis XIII; secretly secretive (to use a worse pleonasm) in Charles II. For Louis XIII kept his plans to himself under a sort of parade of silence, while Charles hid his under an exterior of great openness. And yet it was Louis who could at times be uncertain, and Charles who was inflexible of purpose throughout all the twists and turns in his policy.

In both men also you had the same quality of observation. It was accompanied by high judgment in Charles's case; it was accompanied by a lack of judgment in Louis's which he himself admitted, and which led him to put himself deliberately into the hands of others. But in each it was direct observation; each could pick his man.

And a third quality they have in common is one very manifest when you read of them, and yet so subtle that I almost despair of finding a name for it. It was a quality of separation; not of aloofness, still less shyness or introspection, but a power of putting round oneself a neutral zone, as it were, through which the action of other minds could not penetrate. It was closely connected with a profound appetite for real dignity.

Now, to this parallel must be added the still more remarkable contrast—and it is this contrast, I suppose, which has hidden the fundamental similarity between the two men. For the contrast in action is most obvious. Charles had great humour; Louis XIII none. Charles loved to appear open, and, as I have said, it was the best screen he could have had for his hidden power of intrigue and tenacity therein; Louis XIII almost paraded his avoidance of openness, and used it, as I have also said, like a mask. Charles II was a great lover; Louis XIII was the most singularly unloverlike of any king that ever pretended to a posterity. Charles would not fatigue the body; Louis rode furiously for hours, and was active in every kind of work with his hands, from shoeing horses to sawing wood. Above all, Louis XIII was essentially a soldier: all his interest was in arms, and in that interest he spent his life—which gave him ample opportunity for so spending it. Charles showed neither aptitude nor desire for arms. He was equally courageous, but the military affair did not appeal to him as it did to his brother James; and if he loved men-of-war, it was more with an interest in hulls and rigging, I think, than in tactics; though it is true that his conduct of admiralty was continuous.

But the most lasting (in its effect on history) of the contrasts between the two men was in the matter of public policy and ministerial service. It is the whole meaning of Louis XIII to history that he chose, maintained, and abandoned all direction to, Richelieu. It is the whole meaning of Charles II to true history that he was far superior to any servant and directed his own policy. It is astonishing to observe with what mastery he directed it. He had come back to a dismantled throne, a broken monarchy. He was but the salaried puppet of the richer classes which had destroyed his father. He was overshadowed by the might of his cousin, the King of France. He was heavily pulled at by the United provinces of Holland with their new-found wealth and vigour and their great power at sea. He had to consider at home a large Catholic minority with which he sympathised, and over against it the nation, already in bulk anti-Catholic. He had to govern with instruments which were every one of them potential rebels, and through a gentry which by this time considered itself the heir to the dying kinship and the master of England: a governing class the public expression of which was Parliament. The genius with which he steered between these various forces, estimated the weight of each and the duration of effort in each, played them one against the other, has no parallel save in the action of Richelieu steering between the international forces of a generation before.

But there was this tragic difference between the two masterpieces. Richelieu's work was directed to the grand object of strengthening and exalting a whole society, a nation and its incarnation in the King. Charles's work had for its object nothing more than the precarious maintenance of a position wholly undermined. He desired to die with his half-valueless crown on his head. By dint of genius he succeeded. But his success meant nothing enduring to the things he cared for most, and nothing to the country which he nominally ruled.

Nor could that effort have been maintained. He defeated his worst enemies, he drove out Shaftesbury, he put Russell to death. Yet all his success was on a slope which led towards some necessary and ultimate failure. One can only say that he died in time.

Lastly, let this be noted in the fate of these two men. Each failed to impress himself upon posterity. The figure of Louis XIII remains strange, but not with a strangeness sufficient to have attracted curiosity or to set an enduring problem. The figure of Charles II remains caricatured and unhistorical; in the gallery of the kings both their places are empty, or filled in the one case with a shade, in the other with a false image.

XI

Este

I am afraid the motives which made me turn out of the road to visit Este will seem inadequate to my reader. They were adequate enough for me, for I have a religion towards names and places: a religion intense according to their significance in history. So, because the great house of Este (of which was Queen Victoria) took its title from the little Euganean town, to the little Euganean town I went.

The great house of Este has very different associations. Its roots lay far off beyond the Apennines in Tuscan land, and its lords were little lords amid those dead volcanoes long before they took a title from these other dead volcanoes of the Euganean hills, from the summits of which a man may see very far off to the eastward at morning a mist above the lagoons of Venice. And the destinies of that great house, after it had assumed the Este name, were carried far from Este. The name means rather, to those who know Italy and her story, Ferrara, the glories of the Renaissance and the name of Beatrice: but Este gives the stamp. Just as the mighty name of Montfort springs from that tiny sharp hill hidden away in the forest within a ride of Paris, on the edge of the

Vexin and the approach to Normandy from the south, so does the mighty name of Este spring from the little half-forgotten town and its older castle on the sharp hill above. To Montfort also I went some little time ago, moved by the same feelings which also moves me to visit the springs of famous rivers.

The pilgrimage to Este well rewarded me. It is a good little town, with something left of its most ancient stones and much of its traditions. It is lively, the people are active in commerce and piety, the hotel is kind, and what people call primitive; for I suppose in these days even such very few as care to see Este in their travels do not sleep there, but take it from Padua.

The approach to it by the plain is not to be forgotten, because the vast pyramids of the hills all clustered together, thrown up by the heats of the earth in the beginning of time, stand out utterly different from the dead level all around. If one sees them first in thick weather they almost deceive one into thinking them the works of man, so simple and abrupt is their outline and so wholly isolated are they. It should make the traveller glad that so famous a name should have such a setting, a landscape of so permanent and fixed an effect; for many another great name, Bourbon for instance, has an unworthy setting. Yet you will look in vain, I think, in Este for any great memorial of the generations who were proud to call themselves by its name. For these you must seek the greater cities which they ruled when they had become something like kings and were renowned for centuries throughout Europe.

Two matters distinguish the house of Este beyond any other; its vast antiquity and its standing at the fountain head of the Guelph royal family of England. For through Brunswick and the Guelphs, the Royal family of England was in direct Este descent.

As for the antiquity of that blood, it has about it something awful. It has in this but one rival (I mean only one rival in lineages quite certain and not lost in legend). That rival is the Capetian house, the Royal house of Paris. The Este name is older than the Plantagenets, older than Savoy, older than Aragon, far older than Castile. Charlemagne was not long dead when first those lords in Etruria were heard of, Lambert and Guy. How much earlier their fathers were in the possession of Tuscan villas we do not know. Guy's son, Oberto, lent his sword to Berengarius when that man, claiming through women the blood of Charlemagne also, mastered Italy for a moment and was Emperor. When Berengarius was killed, the Tuscan soldier rode over the Alps and joined the Court of Saxony, serving Otto, he who re-founded the Empire to its hurt but to the glory of his name. Otto made him Count of the Palace, and from those days before the middle of the tenth century, when the Danes were harrying England, before the re-conquest of Spain was launched, in the depths of the darkness, the strength of the new house arose.

Not that they stayed with the German Court, they went back to their origins in Tuscany. But the son of Otto's man called himself Marquis, and though I believe it is not known (or has not been preserved) by what mandate, the title must have been Imperial: it was a Marquisate, that is, an hereditary command for the defence of a frontier, for the holding of a March against the Slav threat beyond the Piave which, within living memory, had almost succeeded. This man's son again, still greater in wealth with new lands added to the old, was a power in Europe. Azzo was his name. He withstood his Emperor Henry the Second. He desired to lift the King of Paris of the day—a noble still weak—to the throne of the Empire. Had he succeeded, what a changed business the business of Europe would have been from that day to now! That is, had he thoroughly succeeded and had the Kings of Paris been able to take root as Emperors; the Capetians dominating Europe from that time to this.

But Azzo of Este failed, leaving a son upon whose name anyone not blind to the great things of history stands at attention. Not only did he gather up in his hands all the new power of his blood, governing Milan in the Emperor's name and seizing Rovigo, garrisoning Este itself and all the country round, subdued to his obedience, but he lived for more than a hundred years—elbow room for the much that he did. And one of the things he did was to marry the daughter of the Guelph, the sister of Carinthia, and so to be called himself a Guelph and to hold the duchy of Bavaria. From him all the Guelphs descend. That is why the name of Este stood at the head of the royal family of England. All Guelphs are really Estes.

He did more than that. His second marriage was with the heiress of Maine, so that this surprising Italian had three feet as it were, one planted on his native Lombard plain, one in the Germanies, one in France. Unfortunately, Maine he could not, or would not hold; the passes of the Alps led him to the Bavarian land, but there was no way to Maine; he sold it. He lived on and on, he saw the death of William of Falaise after all the conquest of England, though William of Falaise was a younger man than he. He saw the death of Rufus. Henry the First was already a man of fifty when this great Azzo died. There had passed before him in that astonishing length of days all the stirring of a new Europe, the thunder of the first crusade, the expansion of the Normans, the beginning of the change in Christendom, the new high politics of the Papacy; and henceforward his children and his children's children, onwards for centuries, were, north and south of the Alps, on the summits of an enduring power. They fought as allies of the Lombard League, yet Barbarossa made one of them an Imperial leader. They helped the pagan comet, Frederick the Second, the Stupor of the world, who so nearly overset the mediæval scheme. All the succeeding centuries were filled with them.

Their end in Italy came with the last of the great changes, and it is pitiful enough to read. Hercules the Third of Este was his title. When the armies of the Republic burst through the Alps under the young Napoleon he fled from the ragged soldiery and took refuge in Venice, to be secure beyond the shallow water and the mud banks. It availed him nothing. By a clause in the treaty of Campo Formio the last powers of the house of Este came to an end. It had the glory of dying the death of Venice. There was no heir; an heiress only, who married into Austria, and so that story ended, save for the Guelph branch which endures.

All those things and a thousand others cling round the name of Este, and by reflection illuminate the little town. I am not sure that it knows its own fame, or rather the fame of those to whom it gave its title. No tourists seem to trouble it. Their motors hoot anxiously down its narrow street, racing in from Padua, struggling through Este market, and racing on to Mantua again. It is preserved by one of those accidents, ironic, uncalculated, which occasionally do good, and usually evil. It was a stage from Padua in the days before petrol and steam. To-day, it is too near for a halting place, too far for a close visit. So its false friends will leave it alone and it will never be famous, which is a blessed thing to say of man or town.

XII

A Dialogue on Movable Feasts

CRASSUS: I presume, dear Torquatus, that with your customary perversity, you are opposed to the very reasonable fixing of these absurd Movable Feasts wherewith our Calendar is encumbered?

TORQUATUS: As is the custom of your cretinous kind, Crassus, you tell both a truth and a lie in one breath: yet in this I do not blame your morals, but your intelligence. I am not perverse, and a man must indeed be suburban to think me so; but I do protest with all my soul against this irreverent tomfoolery of interfering with the Great Feasts.

CRASSUS: My poor Torquatus, I make allowances for you! And of course, no Crank thinks himself a Crank; for it is of Cranks as of the Devil, whom your theologians pretend to exist, and of whom they say that if he could repent he would stop being the Devil—which in my judgment would be a pity. So you Cranks, if you knew you were Cranks, would cease to be Cranks. And pray, is it not perverse to set yourself against all your fellow-citizens?

TORQUATUS: This time you lie without any admixture of truth. The greater part of my fellow-citizens are too brutish to have a feeling one way or the other. Of those who care at all, nine out of ten reverence old things and the memory of the Sacred Days—however faint it may have become. While those who would openly disregard such sanctities are but a nasty little group of Intellectuals and Millionaires with their dependants.

CRASSUS: I shrug my shoulders at you, Torquatus; much as I revere your intelligence, your judgment has become hopelessly distorted.

TORQUATUS: And as for you, Crassus, you are stone blind; would God you were deaf and dumb as well!

CRASSUS: Come, Torquatus, sweeten yourself and listen to gentle reason! Consider the advantage to all our clerks, our employees and civil servants that they should have their Easter in good weather, and should be able to know its date for certain, as they do August Bank Holiday, the Derby, Christmas, and other Sacred Days, as you call them.

TORQUATUS: It is like your insufficient mind to harp upon Easter! It is true that upon Easter the rest are modelled; but do you think that Easter alone is at stake? There is Ash Wednesday, there are the number of Sundays after Epiphany, there is Mid-Lent (with its fattened pig), there is Maundy Thursday, there is Good Friday, there is Low Monday, there is Whitsun, there is Trinity . . .

CRASSUS: I could stop my ears at all this rigmarole of names with some of which not I nor one man in a hundred has any acquaintance to-day, and with the rest of which there stands no reason for changeability. I ask you again, have you considered the advantage it would be to all our folk that they should enjoy Easter in good weather?

TORQUATUS: If they would enjoy Easter in good weather let them go to the Balearics, where it is fine all the year round. But you must be like most of our moderns, drunk with print and unable to use your own five wits, if you have not observed that it is nearly always bad weather in England, and that the luck of good weather has nothing to do with the season. Come, Crassus, have I not heard you yourself mouthing it out that it is the incredible nature of our climate which has made you what you are—in which product you would seem to take a fatuous satisfaction.

CRASSUS: And what of the convenience to the millions of exact budgeting, and knowing beforehand year by year when the holiday is to be taken?

TORQUATUS: Free men ought not to alter their customs for the convenience of slaves.

CRASSUS: Do you call Lord Gubernator a slave?

TORQUATUS: As he now stands, I should rather call him a Libertinus, or slave emancipated and an offensive one at that. At what age did he first use a handkerchief?

CRASSUS: Is it nothing to you that the House of Lords and the House of Commons are agreed on the matter?

TORQUATUS: It is a great deal; for on whatever they decide I hold the contrary opinion.

CRASSUS: Pray, Torquatus, have you reverence for the Ecclesiastical Moon? The Dominical Letter? The Epact? The Golden Number? Do you hold them in a Sacred Awe? Do you recognise in them the dreadful Spirit of the Divine?

TORQUATUS: I will lay my head to a china orange that

you could not say what is meant by the Ecclesiastical Moon, that you cannot define the Epact, that you know not how to arrive at the Dominical Letter for the Year, and that the Golden Number is a mere noise in your ears. Come, I will proceed to instruct you: we calculate the Ecclesiastical Moon as follows: considering the Vernal Equinox as at midnight, not at its actual hour, we next . . .

CRASSUS: Oh, no, my dear Torquatus, we do not! This is getting worse and worse! Of all tomfool abominations, give me the dead dust of clerical technicalities. At any rate, we need not quarrel upon the affair, for all is decided, and without a doubt we shall have a fixed Easter before ten years are out.

TORQUATUS: And pray what has that to do with the issue? We shall very probably have the Plague before fifty years are out, and before a hundred are out the total subversion of our civilisation. But is that any reason why we should approve? Have you then a Sacred Awe in the presence of the Future? And do you think that Wednesday must be of its nature nobler than Tuesday?

CRASSUS: Why, no; but I can distinguish between a practical discussion and futile debate upon settled things.

TORQUATUS: Then why did you begin this wrangle? And why do you, now that the argument turns against you, attempt to cut it short? You remind me of the Nestorian Party at the Council of Ephesus. Or perhaps I should rather say the Egyptian Party; for when I come to think of it, it was they who both started the quarrel and then tried to closure it.

CRASSUS: Now, Torquatus, it is my turn to tell you

simply why you are wrong, and why everyone thinks you are wrong.

TORQUATUS: Two lies this time!

CRASSUS: It is because, in your considerable but eccentric reading, you have lost your way, and no longer live in the time in which it has pleased God to set you.

TORQUATUS: We will, if you please, leave third parties out of the discussion.

CRASSUS: When the Movable Easter arose, men lived very simply, after the fashion of the Dark Ages, and . . .

TORQUATUS: I groan in agony at your ignorance! The Age of the Julian House the Dark Ages! You have never heard of the fourteenth of Nisan! Nor even of the Quartodecimans! Nor of the Johannine Paschal tradition! Yet you talk: you actually *talk*! Why are such animals granted speech?

CRASSUS: . . . it was no inconvenience, but rather a pleasure, to find diversity in the Calendar. Nor did men know then that the Celestial Orbs have no influence upon our lives, as we now know they have not.

TORQUATUS: How do we know that?

CRASSUS: And to the simple work of the fields . . .

TORQUATUS: There is not one single agricultural work you could perform . . .

CRASSUS: . . . it was no disturbance that this dance of the Festivals up and down should appear. But to-day, in our mighty industrial civilisation, where all is worked with precision and by rule, the thing has become intolerable. A Movable Easter is like a cripple hobbling in the middle of a motor way. It must go.

TORQUATUS: And so must you, Crassus. And that quickly, I beg.

CRASSUS: Farewell, Torquatus; I love you the better for your oddities.

TORQUATUS: And I despise you the more for your empty, empty, empty head.

XIII

A Guide to Boring

I AM distressed to note that in the interesting department of Boring (the Latin *Ars Tædica*) no outstanding work has been done upon the *active* side: the science and practice of Boring.

There has been plenty of writing upon the *passive* side, describing the horrors of being bored; and plenty of sound invective against the Bore; plenty of good description of his appearance and (what is more difficult) a few good descriptions of his approach and manner. But I can remember nothing at the moment describing the Art of Boredom: informing such of us (and I am one) as desire to inflict it upon our enemies. The book wants doing; and I would like to drop a few hints on it here.

In the first place, I will beg my readers to get out of their heads (if they have it lodged there) the idea that boring is not to be learnt and practised, because the bores he knows are commonly aimless. That is a great error. I admit that aimless men are often the best bores —the kind of men who would take the prizes in a National Bore Show. I will even admit that the King Bore is usually himself ignorant of his terrible powers.

But for *deliberate* and *intentional* boring you must have a man of some ability to practise it well, as you must to practise any art well.

For Boring may properly be regarded as an art, and in connection with it I shall now enrich you by giving rules for its successful practise. With that object let me recite you the signs whereby you may discover that your efforts have effect.

The first sign is an attention in the eye of the bored person to something trivial other than yourself. If while you are talking to him his eye is directed to a person aiming a gun at him, that is not a sign of boredom. But if you see it directed to a little bird, or a passing cloud, that is a symptom, as the doctor said. Another symptom is occasional interjections which have nothing to do with what you are saying. A third, and very much stronger, symptom which should especially delight you as a proof of triumph is the bored one's breaking out into conversation with somebody else in the middle of your speech.

The choice of subject for boring is of no great consequence. Any subject can be made interesting, and therefore any subject can be made boring; but the method is all-important. And the first rule I would give in this matter is to speak in a sing-song, or at any rate with continuous repeated rhythm and accent. Those perfectly practised in the art can talk rapidly without punctuation and with no raising or lowering of the voice; but you rarely ever get this in its perfection except from politicians, though I have known others who were not bad at it. The chief master of the style, to my certain knowledge, never got into the House of Commons at all; he was only a candidate; but I walked miles to listen to him at his meetings for the sheer pleasure of seeing it done.

Another very useful tip is the bringing in of useless detail, and the branching of it out into a luxurious growth of irrelevance, and this works best of all when you are telling a story which is intended to please by its humour. Thus it is a very good plan to open with hesitation over a date: "It was in July, 1921—no, now I come to think of it, it must have been 1920, because—" (then tell them why it must have been 1920). "No, now I think of it, it must have been 1921"—(then tell them why it was '21)—"or was it 1922? Anyway, it was July, and the year doesn't matter; the whole point lies in the month."

That is a capital beginning, especially the last words, which indicate to the bored one that you have deliberately wasted his time to no purpose.

A parallel method is to worry about a name which you have forgotten, and which is in no way material to your story.

A third tip, and a useful one, is the addition of all manner of local colour and descriptive touches. You must imitate as well as you can (it is not saying much!) the accent of the characters in your story, and you must begin a lot of sentences with "It was one of those . . ." and then pile on the adjectives.

A further rule is to introduce digressions, especially of an æsthetic or moral sort. Stop in the middle of the thing and add to the agony by explaining that you don't mind a man's getting drunk, or that you do mind it, or that you have no objection to such a building as you are describing, or what not: for your private opinions in art and morals are the most exquisitely boring things in the world and you can't bring them in too much.

Again, remember that there are special ways of adding to the effect, of bringing out what may be called the high-lights of boredom. Of these by far the finest is suddenly forgetting the end of your story, just as you are reaching it. It has an enormous effect. I knew one case where a man had a bottle thrown at him because he did this, and no handsomer proof of his success could have been given. The sharpest form of it is to lead your piece of boredom up to a question such as: "And what do you think he answered?" and then you pause a minute and say: "Damn it all! I ought to remember . . . I've almost got it! . . . you see, the whole point depends on getting the words exactly right . . ." Then, after keeping them all in a little hell for thirty seconds, say, hopelessly, that you despair of getting it, and leave it at that.

The man who desires to shine as a bore, and uses this offensive weapon with brio and success, must also learn how to break down the defences. Those who have had to suffer high boredom, and who still have energy left in them, can put up a good fight; it is the duty of all bore-students to be ready for such opposition. Thus there is the defence of suddenly interrupting the borer and talking against him in a new and lively tone. For instance, if he begins: "Do you know Rio? Well, once when I was in Rio . . ." the victim may suddenly disclose a nest of machine guns, shouting, "Rio! Bless you, yes! I know Rio!" then pouring out a spate of Rian recollections and thus mastering the enemy fire by a hose-play of words. There are only two ways of countering this. One is to complain openly that you are interrupted and insist on being allowed to go on with the torture. The other is to let the other man exhaust his ammunition and then riposte yourself with renewed energy.

A subtler form of defence, and a very effective one, was invented by a highly-placed permanent official about thirty years ago. It consists in listening to the borer until he has made his point—or what he calls his point— just at that moment putting on an air of complete abstraction, and after that asking why he doesn't go on. To meet this form of defence it is no bad plan to begin the story all over again. That'll teach him!

But the strongest defence—the one you have to fear most—is that of walking away. Most men who have studied the art of boring take this for a definite defeat. They need not. I know one man at a club from whom people used to walk away deliberately in the middle of his boring-exercise. He met the tactic by going after the quitter and catching hold of his coat, and quite half the time he was successful. But few men have such courage.

Lastly, let me urge on you two private recipes of my own. One is spells of silence in the intervals of boring —it's a paradoxical truth that they add vastly to the effect. They must not be so long as to let the victim take up a book, but just long enough to break his nerve. Watch his face, observe its gradual relaxation, and time yourself exactly for the renewal of the agony. The other is talking half incomprehensibly, mumbling, and the rest of it—then, when the boree impatiently asks you to repeat, do it still less clearly. It never fails.

But all these rules are, after all, mechanical. A man will never become a natural bore by the following of paper precepts any more than he will become a poet by book-learning; so perhaps I have written in vain.

XIV

On Proportion in Building

IF WE had preserved an excellent custom of our fathers, the custom of giving long titles, I would have called this "On Proportion and Scale in Building, or A Disquisition upon the Canons of Architecture in so far as they refer to Ratios of Length, Height and Breadth, as also the Fundamental Elements of Curves," and having done that I suppose I should have added "By Hilaire Belloc, Esq., B.A., sometime Member of Parliament for South Salford, etc., etc., etc.," and then I should have dedicated it to the Rt. Hon. the Earl of Stopham, K.G., F.M.H., D.S.O., O.M., etc., etc., etc., with a long preface, and then he would have paid me a great deal of money. But all this I will postpone until I come to write upon lengthy titles.

Of all necessities in building—I mean necessities of the soul (for the body should be satisfied with any good watertight cave or large tub), Proportion is the first and the main essential. In the lack of it, we are ill at ease; in its presence we are satisfied. Yet the laying down of rules for it has hardly been achieved, or, if achieved, has largely been lost. Its re-discovery sets as difficult a task as any we have given to us to do—and it is a task which very few people seem to be so much as attempting, let alone fulfilling. This is because the instinct for right proportion *is* an instinct. It is organic, not conscious of its origin nor knowing when it is working at its highest.

It would seem, when we look at the works of man in every age before the present chaos, as though canons of proportion, having been somehow or other arrived at, made explicit and crystallised, were formulated as rules and followed empirically. They differed with the varying cultures. What can we discover common to them which may help to guide us back to right sense in these matters?

The first thing that occurs to one, the oldest and the most well-worn of truths in this department, is that in these scales the works of man must have had Man for their measure. A column a yard high is short, a column a hundred yards high is tall, because short and tall in columns are words relative to man. With mere scale this truth is obvious, but with Proportion there enters in something much more subtle, something which makes Beauvais look a great deal higher than the Eiffel Tower, and the Papal Palace at Avignon more imposing in mere mass than any skyscraper. How these effects are produced, many architects with the genius of their craft have explained, and we who know nothing of architecture as a craft and are only writers must not attempt the task. But we can make suggestions.

The test of proportion is satisfaction, but how is that satisfaction to be attained? The quality of proportion resides (almost obviously one might say) in the idea of the Normal—which is wrongly translated "the Mean."

For instance, between the deliberate effects of exaggeration—the excessive in length or height or in shortness or lowness—there is a middle thing which is exactly appropriate to, and in harmony with, the human spirit; something in which we repose; and the achievement of that something depends upon the obtaining of right proportion. The eye is offended by the too highly stilted curved arch. It is, or should be, offended by the flattened one, or if not offended it is at least disturbed. It is fully satisfied by the full and plain half-circle, which is the Heaven under which man moves, and which proclaims equality and sundry other things.

When you marvel, in the crypt of the Escorial, at a vault so flat that you would think it could not stand up, you admire the skill of the craftsman; but you are not in the presence of the normal. When you find, at the end of the Middle Ages, and in their transition to the Renaissance, the stone pendant drooping from the midst of the vault, and are told how it is an ingenious use of the keystone, you admire, as you would a beautiful conjuring trick, but you cannot repose in the sight.

There is one rule which seems to underlie the achievement of the normal, and of true proportion, which has often been stated in various ways, but the re-statement will do no harm. It is this, that the simple geographical figures, the figures which are developed through the plain sweep of a cord, satisfy the eye, and that the figures which are plain multiples also satisfy the eye. It would seem that the shapes which have endured as comfortable habitations for the human spirit are based, all of them, upon this main canon from which the others derive. The arch of a bridge, if it be semicircular, or if it be a fragment of a circular circumference, or even if it be an ellipse (which, after all, is drawn with one simple cord, though turning upon two posts instead of upon one) are examples. Another is the ogive made by two insecting equal quadrants containing an equilateral triangle.

The sphere satisfies, or rather parts of the sphere. Does the cube? It is less successful. I am often puzzled why this should be so, and I have never approached a solution. There are some rare interior cubic rooms which satisfy, and I have seen buildings, especially in Spain, which were based upon the idea of the cube, which were perhaps in their extremities contained by a cube (but were not cubic) and satisfied the eye.

Plain multiples satisfy the eye, and it might be argued that in some cases the relation of the diameter to the circumference of a circle satisfies the eye. I remember reading once in one volume out of the whole library of nonsense upon the Great Pyramid that it contained a relation of this sort. Perhaps the area of the base was to the height as the area of a circle to its radius or diameter; perhaps it was some other two proportions that fulfilled this canon. At any rate, the proportion was there.

Certain other derivatives satisfy even though they are odd; at any rate they do not shock; and these also are derived from the simpler forms arrived at with the compass. For instance, the regular pentagon and hexagon and octagon, not, indeed, in the shape of a window, where they are hideous, but in the division of a round or in the six-pointed star, or the five-pointed, of which the best example I know is in the window of the north transept of Amiens. So also the lancet window set in an angle of eighteen degrees, which is a derivative of the pentagon, satisfies the eye. So also, less satisfactory but tolerable, is the pointed arch set in an angle of 45 degrees instead of an angle of 60 degrees.

What angle satisfies in a roof? I have long puzzled over it, but never arrived at a solution. Certainly it is not the angle of 45 degrees; that happens to be always an irritant, though why I do not know. The noble great roofs of Northern Europe are always steeper, and the Southern are flatter than 45 degrees; it is beyond me, and I leave it at that. But I know that the multiple satisfies the eye, and I should like to sing the praises of the square root of 2, which is full of meaning indeed, and to which I will come in a moment; so stand by.

The plain multiple—e.g. a tall window divided so that it is built up of two or three or four squares; a room twice or three times its breadth in length, and a wall the same—these have a sort of finality so long as the eye can appreciate that it is dealing with a plain multiple and is not deceived by perspective; and it is often true that if you cheat the eye into believing that it is dealing with a plain multiple, it reposes therein. But more subtle and of fuller finality is my treasure, the square root of 2. That also is arrived at in the simplest of fashions. It is the diagonal of the square. Take a tall window, mullioned; let the lower half of it have the proportion of side to breadth as the square root of 2 is to 1; let the upper half of it be a square; then you have, I think, a permanent and established window with which you can live and your children after you. And I believe that the end wall of a room set lengthways in this fashion, so that the height is to the breadth as 1 is to the square root of 2, gives the same sense of completion. And there

81

would seem to be reason for this, for you have here an harmonic. It is the property of a parallelogram in which the longer side is to the shorter as the square root of 2 is to 1, that its half is of the same shape as the whole, its quarter the same shape as its half, its eighth the same shape as its quarter, and so on. Take a piece of paper of these proportions (most notepaper used to be of this shape); you will find that after you fold it the shape is still the same, and if you refold it, still the same, and if you fold it a third time, it is still the same. It is the proportion you come across continually in the buildings of the true Middle Ages, when design was traced on the ground with a cord swinging round a pivot. The proportion "$\sqrt{2}$ to 1" can be arrived at at once on the ground by joining the ends of the perpendicular radius to the end of the horizontal one.

Consider, then, these canons of a layman, all you architects; apply them to your work; and if I know anything of attempts to recover the lost spirit of beauty, you will achieve results most hideous and damnable.

XV

Charles Brandon, Duke of Suffolk

THERE is a whole procession of men, long dead, whom I should like to have met. But of late weeks during my reading I have been filled with a desire to have met Charles Brandon, Duke of Suffolk, more than any. I regret the considerable gap between his death and my birth, more in his case than that of any of his contemporaries.

For one thing, there was no problem. An inspection of, even a close acquaintance with, Charles Brandon, Duke of Suffolk, would never have tired my poor head with analysis of motives, at which game I never was a champion. He was all of one piece, as simple, as ridiculous, as despicable and as entrancing as any adventurer that ever stepped.

He was a barber's block. The ladies fell for it—if I may use an Americanism. He never failed. I have the same sympathy with him as I have for the Duke in *Rigoletto*. When a man is as careless of honour and all the major and minor morals as that, when he goes prancing through life like a two-year-old and keeping it up to sixty, tell me, do you not agree with me? Is it not delightful?

One severe commentator upon this mazurka career has written of him, not quite justly, that he had five wives, of whom the first was his aunt and the last was his daughter-in-law. I could modify the relationships slightly; I don't think it could be proved that Mary Brandon was his aunt, and I don't think that other word "daughter-in-law" is accurate. But both will serve. He was the kind of man who would have married his grandmother if he had seen any advantage in it, and, what is more, he would have carried it off and got on with her splendidly.

That, indeed, was the chief point of the man—carrying things off. He carried them all off. He carried them off their legs. He gets himself entangled when he is barely out of the shell with a Miss Brown, of no particular standing; he gets out of that contract in order to marry Mary Brandon; he abandons Mary Brandon to return to Miss Brown, who is pleased to present him with children. With these ladies in the background he urges Henry VIII, who was obviously fascinated by him, but also bewildered and troubled by the high voltage, that he would be just the spark to marry Margaret, the Emperor's daughter and Governess of the Netherlands. At any rate, let him go as Ambassador to begin with. Off he goes; and the first thing you hear of him is that at dinner he goes down on one knee before the lady's lap, takes her hand, and roguishly slips off her ring. He was not the man to let the grass grow under his feet, and there is no denying that poor Margaret was moved. She had not been lucky hitherto, and brilliant, very handsome, courageous Englishmen of thirty or less who play forfeits suddenly with your rings and bracelets (he got hold of a bracelet after the ring) were a novelty in the stern great world of the Hapsburgs. She simpered not a little. She was reprimanded. She was told by her imperial father that such goings-on "were not the custom of *our* country." She wrote a tearful explanation and apology, all of which you may read with pleasurable interest in the great collection which Mr. Brewer edited before you and I were born.

Meanwhile the excellent Charles, the dashing light-stepper who had carried one of the gates of Tournai with his own hand, and was always ready for the next thing, had been given the Royal title of Duke in prospect of that great marriage which had failed to come off.

But Charles Brandon, now Duke of Suffolk, and able to jostle at ease the exceedingly annoyed Duke of Norfolk, lineage and all, mourned not an hour for Margaret's loss, any more than he had mourned for the humble Mary Brandon or the humbler Brown. Other things were coming his way, as they do come the way of these admirable gallants. The very next year he was off to France to see after the King's interests there and to bring back the King's sister, whose elderly husband, the French King, had just died. The King's sister was nineteen; Charles Brandon, just turned thirty and as merry as ever. Mary Tudor made up her mind at once. She had been a widow long enough. It was several weeks since Louis's death. She proposed in the frank and fearless old fashion to Charles Brandon, and he with superb courage said "Yes."

It was risking his neck. In the days of the Kings you did not become a King's brother-in-law without the

King's leave and off the lady's own bat, as it were, without sailing too close to the wind.

But if ever there was 'a "nothing venture—nothing have," it was the happy Charles, bringing back his equally happy bride, standing for some days between life and death, spared, retiring into a sort of disgrace (as though a man like that could be kept under!) but bound, indubitably bound, to come to the surface again, like a cork. Mary Tudor died, but not before she had given him children, one of whom was the mother of Lady Jane Grey. Indeed, there was already present what Henry had so dreaded when he heard, in his fury, of that marriage—the danger of a new succession.

By the time Mary died (Queen of France as she was always called) the follower of fortune, the man who in any place, high or low, would have carried his sword with a swing, was nearing fifty, and was getting fat. But he carried on, he still carried on. He must have thought to himself that he had not done so badly; he, the grandson of a squire, a man early favoured because his somewhat obscure father had borne the standard for Henry VII at Bosworth and been very properly killed by the last Plantagenet, white-hot against treason. He had collected love affairs in splendid succession, he had neither disappointed nor been disappointed. He had married a Queen, he was brother to a King, he had led more than one triumphant march into the heart of enemy country. Was there anything left for him to do?

There was. The Queen of France was dead, Charles Brandon was a widower. It was a state of life for which he had no more liking than had had the deceased in the day when she had approached him so frankly on his embassade eighteen years before. It was on the 24th of June that Mary Tudor died. On Sunday, September 7th, Charles Brandon married again—for the last time (I think). The lady was Catherine Willoughby. He was the better acquainted with her because she was betrothed to his own son, so all was well. That same day, but some hours later, was born the child who was to be Elizabeth of England.

So Brandon carried on and still carried on, and went on carrying on—an inexhaustible fellow, the mirror of all adventurers and care-free scoundrels. He was not yet tired. He had twelve years to live, and he filled them as full as the other forty-eight, or, let us say, the other thirty-two; for I doubt whether he began his gallivanting before sixteen, though he was capable of anything.

He loaded his pocket with Church loot, sweeping it in with the best of them, and of all those robbers none, I think, carried off their peccadillo so gaily. The Duke of Norfolk might boast of thirteen monasteries, the Percys of eighteen, but Suffolk beat them by several lengths. *His* bag was *thirty*.

He had need of such wealth, for there never was a profligate less avaricious; he scattered whatever money he had all his life, and had something to show for it —resplendent with jewels and cloth of gold even in those days of violent magnificence.

I leave him with regret; I should like to have gone on writing about him, still more should I like to have met him. I should like to have dined with him—after all, he had excellent manners and probably knew how to drink. I should like to have been there when he dined with Morette, the French Ambassador, when the light table-talk turned upon a considerable feast of burning alive which had just taken place in Paris.

The only time when it might have been less pleasant to have been with Charles Brandon would, I suppose, be that moment in which he was first aware that he would die.

★ XVI ★

Bad News for the Expert

THE expert is getting into trouble. He is losing caste. His position is wobbling. "What!" you cry. "Surely he is at the height of his power?" Let me instruct you.

You may make of the power of any institution two curves, or graphs, one red; one green, if you are able to afford coloured inks; one in a full line, the other in a dotted, if you aren't. The one line gives the rise and fall of the institution in its own estimation, and therefore in that of the general world; the other gives the rise and fall of the institution in its secret potential value, the rise and fall of its real effect and power.

The first curve over-shoots the second. The maximum of real power is passed long before the apparent has begun to go down hill. It was so with the English monarchy, for instance. It passed its true peak just after the death of Henry VIII. Its apparent summit comes at least as late as the early years of James I, though it had been rapidly declining in real power all during the reign of Elizabeth.

It was the same with the power of the landed aristocracy of the United Kingdom. Its apparent summit was in the unquestioned time of the mid-Victorian paradise; its real summit came just before the Napoleonic wars, or during them. It will, I think, prove the same with the power of Nationalism. Its apparent summit is in this our very day; probably our children will see that its real summit was passed somewhere about the late eighties of the last century.

Well, so it is with the expert. Never was he so necessary, never did he think so much of himself, never did we think so much of him, as in this happy year 1931. But I guess that he got a secret wound when most of us were still young. I hear grumblings against him. I know that he is being challenged. Indeed—horrible thought!— I believe that some of the great corporations who employ him are not paying him as much money as they did.

Now the reasons for this new and hidden thing (which is certainly present though still unappreciated) are worth examining.

The first cause of the affair, as it seems to me, is the work of Time and his winnowing fan. It takes men long to wake from habit, to sit up and examine fashion, to weigh mere routine, and to grope through the shifting business until they have grasped reality. And therefore it has taken modern men a long time to discover the very simple truth that each of them is an expert. Every man is such an expert in his own life, external and internal, that no scholar in the Ecole des Chartes, nor Egyptologist in Bloomsbury can hold a candle to him. I would bargain to pass an examination on the books and furniture of my study and on the various things which have happened there in the last twenty-five years and to get full marks where no other man on earth could score five out of a hundred.

And this being an expert in one's own job of living, and being an expert therein superior to all the partial experts in the sciences, is of first-rate importance. We are experts in saving and losing our souls; and every sensible man over forty has found out long ago that he is a better expert at saving his body, if that is worth while, than any expert in the art of healing.

Another thing which time has done is to teach men that the accumulation of facts, and even an experience of their working within a strictly limited field, is not only a different matter altogether from right judgment, but tends to be at conflict with right judgment.

Men ought to have found that out long ago, of course; it is a thing so obvious that one ought to spot it at first sight. But we are so made that it takes time to bring the obvious to the surface; and this bit of obviousness has only shown its snout above the water quite lately. However, it has already been seen by a fairly large number of people, and the recognition of it is spreading.

Any fool with industry can pile up expert knowledge of things outside ordinary experience. He need not even have a good memory; he can card-index his facts. But only that rare animal, the wise man, can co-ordinate general experience, give its due weight to each of many different factors in a problem, and see things solidly and sanely.

Expert knowledge (if knowledge it can be called) tends to judge ill. It is at issue with right judgment. Your expert on nervous troubles tends to see the whole world as a mad-house. Your expert on currency tends to forget or to belittle the basic truth that wealth must be produced if men are to live. Your expert on the authorship of pictures becomes quite horribly blind to their beauty. Your expert on dates in history, on documents, comes out blandly with the opinion that his moons are made of green cheese.

It was only the other day that I read a book by a man who had certainly accumulated more facts on a particular historical character (let us call it Gallimogrobus, so as to provoke no quarrel) than any other scholar alive. His footnotes were like a swarm of cockroaches; he had a dozen correct dates to the page—but on the main historical problem concerning this same Gallimogrobus he advanced the enormity that a public man's motive for prolonged and difficult action could not be the fascination exercised over him by a woman, but must necessarily be some Reason of State.

Another expert, a mathematical one this time, has solemnly told us of the electron "that it is at once everywhere and nowhere." While a third, an expert in finance, assures us that never were the economic prospects of this country so rosy.

But I think the worst blow the expert has received he has himself delivered. He has followed, inevitably perhaps, the fatal routine of power. He has sunk to the taking on of mumbo-jumbo.

Not content with being an expert, he would be a hierarch. He must put on the mitre and the long robe, and use a strange tongue. Now, sooner or later this kind of thing gets found out. So long as the expert is content with talking nonsense about things that do not immediately concern us we rather admire the awful process of his ritual. But when he talks of pulling out all our teeth, or preventing our taking a glass of beer, or assures us that we shall soon find hydraulic drills delightful by "adaptation," it is time to look into the matter—and we look into it. And when we look into it we find that the expert through too much flattery and power in the past has become a humbug. His adopted garb of superiority, his technical terms no longer take us in: for externals like dressing-up and using incomprehensible language are no guarantee of authority.

But if the expert is declining (you may tell me) all is lost. In pointing out the horrid truth I play the anarchist. Undermine the expert, and you undermine that delicious place the modern world. Without him we shall be orphans of the storm. He is our only support. Why snatch him away?

Be comforted! The expert shall continue. In fact, he must continue. We have need of him. If all the experts in London were to be struck tomorrow with paralysis, we should have the plague within three days, and general mixum-gatherum afterwards. He will continue all right. But he will gradually lose his position of being our master and will become our servant; if, indeed, our civilisation is to survive, which is something of a begging of the question.

It is a hopeful sign, anyhow, that he is already tending to become our servant rather more and our master rather less. He is, of course, the servant of a few rich men rather than our own; but that general consciousness which, while it does not govern, is at least the air we breathe and the thing which inwardly forms us all, is in revolt; incipient revolt, but revolt. The stories told by the experts were fun as fairy tales. The fun got sombre when it was no longer a question of fairy tales but of the break-up of home, the degradation of human life, and the inculcation of despair. When the expert was entertaining us with statistics on life and death we were interested, but when he went on to make laws for sterilising us or preventing our getting a glass of beer we began to question him. The reaction against the expert has started. As with all other great revolts and all other great reforms, it may be conducted to a wise issue or to a disaster. For my part, I shall be dead long before the crisis comes; but if I were there, I should give my vote for preserving the expert and even for raising his average salary—which, as I said at the beginning of this, is beginning to sag alarmingly.

XVII

On Being in the Limelight

I FANCY men are divided into two sorts: a very large majority who in very different degrees like being in the limelight—from those on the right or violet end of the spectrum, who would just as soon be talked about as not, to those at the deep red end, with whom notoriety is a consuming passion; and of these there is a small minority to whom it is an abomination, like toothache, or a blow in the face, or prolonged insomnia, or a dread of madness, or the sudden loss of affection, or any other intolerable thing.

It is not to be pretended that this minority which hates notoriety is normal. It does not consist of men who, though in small numbers among their fellows, are to be commended for feeling a sentiment which is, after all, human, natural and right. No. The man who cannot bear publicity, who hates it with a fierce hatred, who flies from it as from a forest fire, is not pursuing the ends of his being. He is a crank, and there is no excuse for him—except that cranks must needs be, even to their own destruction and suffering.

The proof that this is so, is, that your normal man even, though he have but a faint or hitherto unaroused appetite for being the subject of other men's attention, takes it for granted that anyone in the limelight is worthy of the attention he receives. He also takes it for granted that, other things being equal, it is a pleasure as well as an advantage to have the lantern beam turned full on to one's own weak face.

And another proof that only your crank fears publicity is the way in which very young men look at the affair. Even those who make themselves ridiculous in age by their hatred of advertisement would, when they were very young, have thought public recognition an enviable thing. I never in my own trade met a young man yet who had not, when he first saw his name in print, felt a thrill of pleasure. I certainly did. It was from the top of a bus in Charing Cross. I saw it on a poster in the year 1890.

There is perhaps a third kind of man who does not mind the limelight, who, when he gets plenty of it, even finds a natural pleasure in it, but who has now got *blasé*. This kind of man may, of course, turn into a furious hater of publicity if publicity pursues him; but as like as not he will only remain mildly opposed to it and avoid it with discretion.

Such a man having been, for instance, a much-discussed Cabinet Minister, or the chief actor in a well-known trial, or perhaps a reprieved murderer coming back out of prison into the world again, will still feel some lingering pride in the great place he once held; but he has had his fill of it, and is willing enough to repose. If now and then chance visitors turn up to call upon him with deference in his quiet country retreat, he is not unflattered, though he begins to get a little annoyed when they come more than once a week.

The man who treats the limelight like poison, being a crank, is comic. He can be comic in two ways: either through his antics and subterfuges, when he is well known and people are really trying to thrust his name forward, or through his absurd exaggeration of the place he really holds, and his idea that he is a public man when he isn't one at all.

About half a generation ago there was a peer of this sort who got it into his head that his title was in everybody's mind, though as a fact not one in a thousand of his fellow-citizens had ever heard it. He would never take a train till after dark, and even then he would pull a soft hat down well over his face on the platform. He was not rich, yet he bribed guards heavily to keep him alone in the carriage, and sometimes he would reserve a whole carriage for himself. When he walked in his gardens, if he thought he heard a vehicle going past the lodge he would dart into the bushes—which, by the way, were rhododendrons (that I may add verisimilitude).

But the greater part of those who dread publicity are right in their dread, because they are very well known, and, if they did not take precautions, would find themselves in the full tortures of the glare.

One of the greatest of the poets of my youth so suffered from the attention of strangers that he built himself a high garden wall; but this did not completely protect him, for the little boys of the place used to put ladders against it and sell for a penny to enthusiastic tourists, especially those who had come from overseas, the right to mount these ladders and peep over at the

Genius. Other men too famous I have known to adopt the bolder method of going about as someone else.

I knew one such myself. He was a great American artist, and he had fled from the world to the desert; that is, to the part of Paris which lies between the Luxembourg Gardens and the river. There he had a tiny little set of two rooms and was at peace. Now I suddenly met this man, whom I greatly revered (and whom I will call Bugg). He was a hero to me, as the famous old are to the infamous young. I came full upon him on the river pavement of the Quai Voltaire, and I said, in a startled welcome, "Oh, Mr. Bugg!"

He looked me full in the face with his dark, melancholy eyes, not discourteously nor unkindly, and said, in his silvery voice:

"*Pardon, M'sieur. Je ne suis pas Mister Bugg. Votre erreur est naturelle. On me prend souvent pour Mister Bugg. Il paraît que je lui ressemble.*"

He bowed, took off his hat with a flourish (thereby disclosing his quite unmistakable hair), and so passed off in his loneliness.

With very rich men, when they suffer from this terror, it is mixed up, of course, with that more rational terror, that someone may bite their ear, touch them, or whatever may be the modern slang for borrowing money. I knew one such man who was the kindest and best of hosts. He is dead now, or I would not speak of him, but I am sure no one will recognise him. He was, I say, the kindest and best of hosts—yet on account of his great wealth he had surrounded himself with barricades and was only to be reached as are giants in fairy tales. When you got at him you found him full of knowledge on quite a number of things, but especially Ivories and Burgundy.

This man gave me a card which he had had printed when he was young, and which moved me greatly. There was his name on it—a symbol for vast wealth—and in the corner, engraved in beautiful small lettering: *"I will take a drink, but I will not lend you money."*

To the honour of rich men as a whole, I think it may be said that they do not fear the limelight, though not many of them take a strong delight in it: they have other things to amuse them.

As for those who feel a consuming passion for the limelight, it is the custom to deride them. But, after all, we only deride them as we deride a man for any human frailty. It is a natural frailty this, even when held in excess. And I, who love my fellow beings, have not infrequently gone to a public meeting (though that is an exercise which I generally avoid) for the pleasure of seeing some Cabinet minister wallowing in the limelight and getting filled chock-a-block right up to the tonsils and back teeth with the intoxication thereof. When I thus take an evening off to enjoy the beatitude of my happy brother, it gives me an added pleasure to recall his origins: the steps by which he has risen to the sublime height on which he, for the moment, stands. I think of his long dark watches on the hard wooden bunk, or staggering along the decks by night in North Atlantic weather on his way to look after the cattle between Canada and Liverpool. Or I think of him going as a super on to some obscure stage, saying, "The carriage waits, m'Lord!" then going out, putting on his rags again, and drawing his half-crown. Or I think of him delivering passionate temperance addresses from a chair at the corner of a muddy street. And then I think of him in all the fever of his election. And then I think of him as I knew him after he got into Parliament, first accepting those rebuffs and insults which it is necessary to accept in the stony way to the limelight. And then I think of the first £150, how it became a thousand, and then of how the five thousand came, and when the twenty-thousand mark was touched. And how that useful tip on the Stock Exchange brought it up to a really substantial amount which made him free. And now here he is, out of the wood and into the limelight, and I am hearing his speech, and though it will be very bad as a speech and will read like nothing on earth, yet because he is soaked through and through with the felicity of the limelight there will be in the delivery of it something, I know not what, which will greatly please me.

The pleasure politicians take in their limelight pleases me with a sort of pleasure I get when I see a child's eyes gleam over a new toy.

But to all this pleasure which I have, one mighty pleasure is added, which caps it all and makes it perfect —the secret pleasure I take in knowing that I am but one of the hundreds of thousands of little white blobs of faces, and that I am not myself upon the platform.

XVIII

An Album of Contrasts

I SHOULD like to have printed and published, for the delectation of the wise, a nice illustrated catalogue with full descriptions showing what has been lost to us in the way of beauty during the last four hundred years through the vices and follies of mankind. It would be a most useful book as a corrective. It might be distributed by any patriotic (or even decently human) patron to revolutionary clubs, parliaments, architectural societies, and the rest of it. Though it were restricted to the last four hundred years, and less—even if it only began with the Wars of Religion in the sixteenth century and went on to the ruins of the last great war—there would be enough to make a mighty volume.

There the reader might see the great tomb of William the Conqueror at Caen—at the beginning of the affair —utterly swept away by the Huguenots. There he might see all the statues round the tomb of the Avignon Pope, whose name and title I forget, but who was buried splendidly on the mountain top in the Chaise-Dieu, equally destroyed by the Huguenots. There he might see the various pictures by the Great Masters of Italy which adorned Whitehall, and which were burned by order of the Long Parliament. There he might see the old Hôtel de Ville of Paris, which went in the Commune; the Tuileries, which went in the same little disagreement on economics; the old Castle of Heidelberg as it was before the French armies destroyed it. But in such a collection he would not find, though it might very well have been there, that immortal waxen head of Lille, which they say was made by Raphael, and which, at any rate, was saved by being buried underground in 1914. There he would find the glorious tower of St. Vaast, in Arras, now dust. There he would find the mediæval cathedral of Orleans and its sister of La Rochelle, both ruined in the religious wars.

It would be no bad plan to have this great book (which might be called *The Book of Example and Warning*) divided under the various motives of folly and crime: the losses due to the hatred of whatever is beautiful or gives joy; the losses due to plain war; the losses due to avarice; the losses due to a breach in tradition; the losses due to the disappearance of taste; the losses due to sloth.

Where engravings of the originals were lacking we could have fairly good restorations made. For instance, one could trust Mr. Griggs to give an admirable etching showing what was once Reading or Osney or St. Edmunds or Abingdon, and what was once St. Paul's.

And, by the way, talking of St. Paul's, would one have a right to put in losses by such accidents as the Great Fire of London? Or by a thunder-stroke such as that which destroyed the tallest steeple in Europe above Ludgate Hill? I think not. For there is no example or warning in accident, unless it is accident due to sloth.

Side by side with these losses, amply illustrated, of the destruction which vice and folly have wrought, with their ruin of beauty, it would be no bad thing to have a corresponding catalogue, well illustrated, of the contrary; that is, of the hideous and stupid and disgusting things which mankind has created in the place of the lovely things mankind has destroyed.

Here there would be only one difficulty—the difficulty of choice. There are in any one of the great capitals of Europe to-day at least a thousand first-class examples of abominations, beginning with the seventeenth century and broadening in an increasing flood to the very moment in which we now live. They are growing up around us upon every side in a profusion never known till now.

Now I come to think of it, it would be an excellent thing to have these horrors side by side with, or opposite, their counterparts. One would say, for instance, "Here is the old thirteenth-century church of such and such a village in Picardy as it stood in 1913. And here is the iron and cement thing which has been erected in its place." Or one might have, opposite such a Griggs etching as I have suggested for Osney Abbey, the gasometer and the railway approach which have replaced Osney Abbey and are the present entry to Oxford. One might have, opposite some pleasant coloured print of Lambeth from the north bank of the river in the year 1800, a photograph from the same point to-day. Or one might take Canaletto's view down the river towards St. Paul's from Westminster, a surprisingly beautiful thing, and have side by side with it another photograph with Hungerford Bridge and the hotels,

Charing Cross Station, and the Shot Tower—not omitting the advertisements.

The idea is capable of extension. For instance, one could have, side by side, on opposite pages, a modern newspaper leader (preferably some leader from the popular evening press written in times of national excitement), and print opposite it one of the nobler and more serene passages of English prose. One could fill a page with the opening lines of the Fourth Book of *Paradise Lost*, and print pretty well any modern poet opposite it, but preferably one of the more obscene and degraded kind.

Then there are faces—one could have a perfect feast with these. You could have on the one side of the page the strong, the subtle, the lively and the sublime, features of thirteenth- and fourteenth-century carving; and, on the other, photographs of various gentlemen and ladies, choosing with loving care the vacuous, the self-sufficient, and the bovine. I would suggest, as a particular example, the head of St. Louis from the western front at Rheims, and opposite it, by way of contrast, the portrait of that great modern which the absence of any law of libel prevents my mentioning—I say the "absence" because the whole point of that department of police to-day is its calculated lack of definition. And, talking of that, another very fine set of contrasts would be excerpts from the virile criticism native to our fathers on one side of the page, and on the other the pap with which we are content to-day. One might take a page from Cobbett—I should suggest one taken from *The Letters to Parsons*, and print it on the left-hand side; opposite it, on the right, one might print any one of those flabby pieces of nonsense beginning with, "though, of course, I do not for one moment doubt the sincerity of my opponent," or "surely it is more charitable to believe."

Personally, I should also enjoy a nice little set of contrasts between the old-fashioned definite conviction and the new-fashioned blur. I remember a passage from Macaulay (though I can't remember where it comes from) in which he grows dithyrambic in his delight at factory chimneys. It begins with the word "Fools" and runs something like this: "Fools said then, as they say now, that the change was for the worse." It would make a very good extract to illustrate what I mean, and opposite it one might have the opening words of some religious article in a Sunday paper.

But the best would still be the most obvious and the most commonplace, the contrast which we all delight in—the contrast in clothes. And here one would have to be very careful, for there were strong men before Agamemnon and there was ludicrously ugly clothing even before our time. One might take the most dignified moment of the later eighteenth century, choosing some handsome type at that, and put the modern stuff opposite it; or one might take a Tanagra to set off a snapshot from the Lido.

But the collection will never be made, and the book will never be issued. Good things never happen. Or, to be more accurate, and to quote and translate the famous lines that were written in the Manor house of Vauvenargues under the mountains of Provence, "Things do not happen. Or, if they do, not at that moment when they would have yielded us the uttermost of delight."

XIX

The Old Palaces

I AM about to take my leisure for some days upon the Continent of Europe, passing from capital to capital, and my chief pleasure will be, I hope, to contemplate the Old Palaces of the Kings. Therein do I find more than in any other splendours a mixture of magnificence and repose, with just that isolation necessary for the soul when it should turn inwards and marry visible things to the invisible.

The Old Palaces were the fruit of one not very long season in the story of the European spirit. They began with the Renaissance; they ended with the Revolution —three hundred years only from the beginning to the end, or barely more. They died, as all good things die; but, as only good things do, they have left in that death a great benediction behind them.

Why should this be? Why should our contemplation of that particular luxury have the spiritual value which undoubtedly attaches to it? It ought not to be so! The Palaces were the scenes of every folly and of every vice, of every injustice and of every vanity, not infrequently of cruelty, always of unbridled appetite or anger, and necessarily of that most despicable thing, man's self-sufficiency and pride, whereby he tries to take the place of God and comes to think of his fellows as other than himself. Yet a spirit has preserved them, as it has preserved no other monuments of mankind, and there is not one—no, not one, of the many that I can count off in my memories—which does not satisfy me fully each in its own way.

Many more lovely things in stone, and perhaps many more majestic, have been set up by the genius of our race. In all of them save the Old Palaces there inhabits a spirit of activity and conflict, exaltation or agony, something alive, even in the last ruins of them. The ruined castles are like prostrate figures of dying warriors, or of strong men in an uneasy sleep, or of the mighty dead captains who might awake; or, where they survive intact, they are like the erect and challenging figures of armed leaders who have been transformed by magic into immobility, but who might in a moment, at a trumpet call, awake. Of this sort are the great strongholds which still continue or have been restored.

The great churches are thronged with a crowd of life, for it is not only the life of this world, but of the other, or perhaps of many others. Such emotions have passed within them, such strength of the spirit was commonly put forth by those who built them, always by some of those who were moved in them, in countless numbers, to remorse, despair, yearning, vision, beatitude, that they vibrate with all this, and the more as time goes on. Even in ruins the great churches give the challenge of life, as the castles do. Stand under the mighty arch of Glastonbury, one thing alone in the air, the last left of so much magnificence; or stand on the lawn wherefrom rises the last ogive of Walsingham, or see the broken height of Bec in its Norman valley; and you will feel life about you almost as strongly as you will feel it in the living shrines of Christendom. Also they go back to an immemorial age. Have I not known such things of the soul in that small square room of Poitiers where the Christian mysteries were already celebrated sixteen hundred years ago?

Even the private houses, such few of them with any antiquity as remain, harbour these unseen forces of life.

But the Old Palaces have a different air about them altogether. One cannot hear, as one walks alone through their deserted gardens, through their empty halls, even the whisper of life actual, but only the memory of living voices; and even these address one in a tone of conclusion and of consummation, as men may speak after the successful accomplishment of a task, or as a sad but noble voice may murmur at the end of a long day done, upon the approach of sleep.

From the Escorial, not abandoned, the noblest of them all, to the last stones of Marly, from the ruin of Heidelberg, from the dignity of Compiègne, all these abandoned things bear witness.

They rise upon the foundations of fortresses built for war. A larger time allowed them, just as the Middle Ages ended, to put on a new grace and a quieter and more exalted glory. Also may you see, in how many places, a mixture of the two—fortress and the home— Amboise, Elsinore. They turned into habitations of splendour or of pleasure, they forgot arms, they became at last the expression in brick and stone and marble and slate of that worshipped monarchy, that Kingship, which was the incarnation of a people, that sacramental union between the mass of citizens and their representative, human idol, which idea ruled the minds of men from the last days of the true European unity to the prodigious crash a century ago, and to the shouts of the revolutionary armies and to their trumpets and their drums.

But in between, during these short three hundred years, all that could be put forward of majesty was set down for posterity to inherit—and to-day from its loneliness it is the more majestic. Some of them war, civil or foreign, has ruined or destroyed. St. Cloud has thus disappeared. Others the accident or catastrophe has left so sharply abandoned that even their quality of greatness seems impaired by too violent an absence of function—it is so with the great Royal buildings of Vienna and its Imperial suburb.

But in the main they still stand for us to visit and to hold full communion with that mood wherein are combined glory and satisfaction and the expectation of the end. They are well suited to great sunsets and to a solemn distant music.

Their noble water pieces are best ornamented by the drifting leaves of autumn; their cornices and balustrades are best framed by those high trees which were planted in the youth of these things so formally, which must in their first years have seemed so bare and small, but which stand to-day like aged gods, and testify to completion, to fruition, to fullness of being at the close.

Nothing of all this will return. And yet the Old Palaces are a promise that man can do such things, in spite of his abominable shortcomings.

They ceased suddenly. Their successors are despicable: things to be avoided: more degrading to those who contemplate them than the worst of industrialism itself. For I would rather look down on the plan of Lancashire from the hill of Glossop upon a murky evening than upon any sham palace of the nineteenth century—a palace of compromise; a palace of the false pretence that something remained of what the fierce flame, in twenty short years between the Bastille and Jena, burned away and destroyed.

Men debate upon the value of the institution of which the Old Palaces were the setting, true monarchy; that late flower of Christendom; that thing which was not there until the chief crowns had established themselves in some security through the religious wars. There are enthusiasts in Europe not a few (and among those are many of the best brains) who would have monarchy restored. They turn with passionate regret to a time which in their secret hearts they know can never return as it was. There are more men still, among those whose right judgment of beauty and of goodness exacts our respect, who find in that brief epoch of monarchy more evil by much than good. I debate not for the moment which of the two schools be right; but somehow monarchy did stamp itself with unmistakable grandeur and justice upon these creations of the human spirit; and profoundly grateful am I and glad that it should so have done. For during my remaining time at least the Old Palaces all up and down the west will be there to receive me when I desire to walk alone and to feel myself a companion with silent peers.

XX

In Praise of Ignorance

ERASMUS wrote in praise of Folly. I, coming exactly four hundred years after, would like to write in praise of Ignorance. I would like to write a little book about it, just as he did about Folly; but I am most unjustly handicapped. In the first place, I can't write what I like because we are not free, as the men of the Renaissance were free; in the second place, I haven't the time; in the third place, I haven't the talent. Still, I can at any rate write a little article in praise of Ignorance; and, so help me God, I will.

Remark the scope and amplitude of the affair! Let any man, however learned he may think himself, however varied his acquaintance with men, muck, money and the printed word, set down a list of subjects on which he could competently deal. Then let him compare it with the cast, the oceanic, prospect of the things of which he knows nothing. Nor let any man be humbled by this comparison. It is a great thing to possess a true knowledge of one's own ignorance, for in a sense you must have knowledge even to know the names of things which you do not know; as for instance, by pairs, Metabolism and Eutychianism, Isostatics and the Greater

Lymphatics, Chronology and Entomology; to say nothing of Apology in the sense of arguments in defence of religious doctrine, for Apology to a Policeman is every man's affair.

You may take a list of countries of which you know the name and the shape on the map, but of themselves nothing at all; of towns, of persons—very great persons whose names are familiar to you, but beyond the name nothing.

To go back to the -ologies, examine yourself on Genealogy. What were the maiden names of Charlemagne's four great-grandmothers? Who is the rightful King of England at the present moment if (and here again glorious Ignorance intrudes) the supposed but doubtful will of Henry VIII still have force of law? What were the claims of the Spanish Infanta to that same throne of England at the end of the sixteenth century? And who was the father of Zebedee's children? Anyone could write down at top speed in half an hour more points of this kind on which he knew nothing than he could write down by laborious self-examination in a whole day similar points on which he had some little knowledge.

The modern system of examination (already menaced) has been very justly blamed by the wisest and the best. One of the less wise and not so good shall here say something in its favour. Anyone who has sat for an examination has had a vivid revelation of his own ignorance. I have written answers to perhaps a hundred examination papers in my time, and my attitude towards each of the wreched printed things as it lay before me

(I being then surrounded by dozens of other victims each at his little desk, with an underpaid Invigilator glaring at us from a platform above) was one of violent bewilderment, loss of foothold, sinking into the abyss. I would see something like this: "Discuss the action of Berengarius at the Council of Blois." I knew vaguely what "Council" meant; I had been to Blois; but beyond that—stumped. Or again, "Give the principal attempts at the trisection of the plane angle by the epicycloidal method." I could not do so. Or again, much more straightforward, "Mention in their order the places visited by St. Paul in his nth missionary journey." Nothing doing.

I say that the soul receives great profit by correction of this kind. No man who has been examined but has at least come upon the knowledge of his own ignorance, which is the beginning of learning. There are some, indeed, so strong-hearted and so sane that they approach examinations daily from the very standpoint of ignorance, like those bluff travellers who, meeting the aristocracy of a foreign land, grin openly at them for mountebanks, keep their end up superbly in the vast saloons of Rome, of Warsaw, of Vienna, and go out contented with a smile yet broader than that which dignified their entrance. Of such was the young student of Divinity (later possessed of a cure of souls in the Isle of Man and quaintly affecting mediæval customs) who, being set a certain examination paper to test his qualifications for Holy Orders, read its terms very carefully and discovered that of six questions he was to select three. Of those six questions one-half meant nothing to him whatsoever; they mentioned things of which he had no more heard than had the Colossians or Ephesians, or whoever they were, of the first century yet heard of the Holy Ghost. But the other three contained each a word which he had heard before: he carefully put a little cross against each such question. They were as follows:

(1) What do you know of the Council of Chalcedon?

(2) Was Sozomen justified in his treatment of the Apollinarians?

(3) What is the distinction between the Cyprianic and the Augustinian attitude towards the Western Patriarchate?

He wrote each of these questions out in a fair, round, clerkly hand, leaving a little space below each. Then, in each of these spaces, he solemnly wrote, for the first the answer "Nothing"; for the second "No"; for the third "None." Having thus completed his paper, he went up and presented it to the Invigilator, bowed, and walked out. The fledgling clerics around him envied the facility of his erudition, the rapidity of his completed task, his early liberation into the happy sunlight of an Oxford June; but he was ploughed.

As is my most unfortunate foible in the discussion of any matter truly profound, I have allowed preliminaries to take up nearly all my space, and I have not as yet approached that chief spiritual attribute of Ignorance, which is its power to flood the mind with happiness. Ignorance is a very draught of beatitude. All the mystery and marvel of a wide champaign seen from a height at evening depends on our ignorance of the nasty people by which it is inhabited, their tortuous and sordid ways. All our loves, all our hero-worships, all our dreams of coming peace, all our visions of fortune, are the fruits of ignorance.

A man leaves a congenial company with whom he has held full communion. He goes off to take his train and thinks to have left behind him souls still vibrating in harmony with his own. They recollect him with a peaceful love. If they return to his name it is with murmurs of approbation. He rolls home satisfied. But the root of his happiness lies deep in ignorance, for hardly had he shut the door behind him when one of them said, "Does he still drink?" And another, "Yes, but he's got to that stage when he doesn't show it." And a third, "That's the most dangerous time!"

Nay, to conclude upon a note of grandeur, it is by Ignorance alone that we advance through the rough seas of this our mortal life. (The metaphor is not original; I do not claim it so; I copy it from others.) Were not men ignorant of what lay before them, no one would face the adventure. I knew one man, indeed, who was quite offensively stupid, dressed in a sort of purple-grey, and had himself so groomed and set up that he looked like the Successful Business Man of the Advertisements—which, indeed, he was. This man told me during a public luncheon that he had found life increasingly pleasant, and that in every fresh stage of it he discovered a further satisfaction. Now, I am glad to say that within twenty-four hours he was shot out of his motor-car and broke upon the sacred flints of England that prominent jaw which he had so abominably abused. Never more would he boast; or at least, not without a horrid mumbling.

In consideration of all this, I thank God for my own Ignorance, and though it is unfortunately less than that of most people, I flatter myself it will serve.

XXI

Laud on the Scaffold

I⊤ was Friday the 10th of January of the year 1645, and
in the morning of the winter day, before it was light,
that William Laud woke from a deep and quiet sleep,
which had refreshed him, though he knew it to be the
last sleep of his life.

He was a man of dreams, and often would he note
them down in that Diary of his which lying enemies
defaced, but which has survived. He had the due reverence of the scholar for visions and for omens. He had
seen in dreams the fate of his friends and had had
warnings all his life long. Whether some vision came
to him in that last night we know not. He betook himself to prayer.

The nature of the death that was before him was
strange enough. He had had his opportunity for flight:
he had refused it. He had thanked Grotius by proxy
for the promised reception. He knew in his heart that
those who hated him would have been relieved by his
disappearance unhurt. Must we admit that in his re-
fusal to fly there was some pride, and a determination
that in this also his opponents should be baffled? Perhaps
a little: perhaps there was an ingredient of this; in his

own words there is something of it. "They shall not be gratified by me in that which they appear to long for." But the very next sentence shows what was deeper down in his heart. "I am almost seventy years old, and shall I now go about to prolong a miserable life?"

That had been months before, and he had remained steadfast. The Scotch clamouring for his blood, the organised rabble of the City through whose insults and threats he was dragged, had ceased to affect him.

He might have refused to defend himself as he had refused to fly. Yet defend himself he did, not before the majesty of a great assembly, but before two or three wearied men sitting on the empty benches, a remnant of the remnant of the Lords. It was not that defence, but sheer necessity, which made them fall back on the universal method of political killing in that generation of England and of its fathers for two generations past: a sentence without pretence of law. Such of the Commons as still remained had voted for death by an ordinance; and, of a score of such of the Lords as still remained, half a dozen may have voted the death of the old man. And indeed his blood had been promised to the Scotch.

He knew also that the bestial affair of half-strangling, castration, disembowelling while the man was still alive, the tearing out of his heart, and all the other details that went with the softening of manners and the broadening of enlightenment in that day, were to be spared him. The old man was to die swiftly, by the axe.

He feared death. That little body of his, quick, vital, intense, would not easily accept the sudden cessation of its functions, warned though it was and holding a soul disappointed in all things save, of course, in its divine assurance.

Moreover, on that cold winter morning, in the small stone room beneath the deep embrasured window, and alone, the old man, long kneeling in careful prayer, was sustained by another kind of assurance: not only of the divine purpose of mercy and security in immortal things, but in his own conviction of right doing. It was a great strength for him. If he had ever wavered in such conviction he would not have had that strength at the end.

They led him out from the half-darkness of the prison into the day. His little peaked face, with the bright, intelligent eyes, and the vigorous, lively, uplifted brows (the men of the time had a fashion in such expression: Bouillon had shown it, and the more controlled and regular Richelieu), was ruddy in the cold morning under its close-cropped white hair, the little white moustache twirled up, the white beard peaked, the eyes, the gesture, the manner, even after all these dreadful months, most full of life. I can believe that he glanced with still awakened interest to the left and the right; he to whom all life had been a theatre of perpetual activity.

He saw before him, dense in the great open space of Tower Hill, as large a pack of upturned faces as even the worst scenes of that London had yet gathered, far more than could crowd into the narrower space round the last low scaffold in Whitehall when, four years on, Laud's master also was to die: he of whom the Archbishop had said that he neither would be great of himself nor allow himself to be made great. (But he meant by those words, Great in power, as a Prince; not great in soul, as a man. For on that Laud had no doubts of his master.)

So they had all come to see that sight, which is not seen every day—an Archbishop of Canterbury put to death as a criminal, but without sentence of law.

He did not stand a singular and isolated, still less an impressive, figure on the rough planks: he was but one in a jostle. Against the usual custom the scaffold was crowded; perhaps because they might fear the effect of his speaking. Nor was Laud agreeable to such a company. He said that he had thought there would have been "an empty scaffold, where I might have had room to die," and then he added, "I beseech you, let me have an end of this misery, for I have endured it long."

Through the planks on which he stood, hurriedly put together (it may be presumed), broad chinks showed, and so densely packed were the populace that even there, beneath his feet, he could see the faces upturned. He bade those about him remove, if it were possible, the people so crowded below, lest innocent blood should fall on them.

He had come to the block, and he began to speak. He spoke in a measured voice, well heard, and having in his mind his supporting Latin phrase, that he "desired to be dissolved and to be with Christ."

I have no space to print here all that we have in the report of those last famous words, but I will set them down as I have read them, choosing out of them what seem to me the strongest.

He told them that the time was not one "comfortable" in which to preach; that he had come to the end of his race to find the Cross—that is, a death of shame. "I have been long in my race, and how I have looked unto Jesus, the author and finisher of my Faith, He alone knows."

Then he spoke of this passage through death, in the knotted metaphors of the time, as a passage through a Red Sea, and therefore, as he trusted, to a Promised Land. But he said, in the midst of that artificial phrase, words memorable for their simplicity and truth: the words of a man who does not hide his heart from his fellows. He confessed the shrinking of the flesh: "I am not in love with this passage through the Red Sea, for I have the weakness of flesh and blood plentifully in me." Indeed, he had, as also its activity and strength, this short, square, sturdy, determined little man.

But as he himself openly acknowledged that fear of death (and the French poet has written how God himself feared Death), he bade all those who heard his aged but resolute voice to the edges of that vast assembly remember that each of them also must come to die, and bade them make ready for the passage. Then he busied himself quietly enough with the details of what was next to be done, the sign to be given for the axe to fall. He knelt, and in one more short prayer still used the twisted language of his time, and its metaphor: but in the midst of this he again enshrined a clear phrase among the rest—a prayer for England.

They let him remain silent for a few moments, the wood supporting his neck, his old head bowed and ready for the stroke, until that silence was broken by a signal agreed, which was in these words, spoken loudly, "Lord, receive my soul." But one dull stroke was needed, and, between his hands, the executioner held up the head, bleeding, before the host assembled.

★ XXII ★

On Lengthy Titles

I THREATENED a little while since to write on Lengthy Titles. I now fulfil my threat, or "implement" it, as the pedants say. I give it curves, which mean beauty. I release it. The blow shall fall. I will write about the Lengthy Title and its advantages; for it is all packed with advantage, and it is a grievous thing that we should have abandoned it. I trust it will return. No doubt moderns are too hurried and too superficial to be troubled with it; it is therefore lost. The lengthy title is not only a just introduction to all that follows it, but a noble and a worthy one, and the snippy title is a poor, undignified thing.

What comfort I derive when, entering an old library, I pick up a solidly bound book, printed in that good clear type of our grandfathers' time, upon paper made of rag, and therefore destined to endure like the cloak of a saintly beggar; a book with one of those lengthy titles which dignity demanded of old. "God's Dreadful Judgment Against the Sin of Lying: exemplified with many Illustrations from Sacred and Profane Writers; to Serve as a Warning to Youth; adorned with Numerous Woodcuts. By the Rev. Joseph Poulton, D.D.,

Sometime Fellow of Magdalen College, Cambridge, Regius Professor of Pastoral Theology to that University, Domestic Chaplain to His Royal Highness the Prince of Saxe-Dittingden, Carey's Prizeman," etc., etc., etc.

That is the way to fire off your cannon! That is the stuff to give them (if I may use so undignified an expression in so high a connection)! Your short title tells men nothing; it adds, therefore, to its failure to use what it fails in decorum, and it is often downright untrue. The old, old joke about *"Mill on the Floss,* ditto on *Political Economy,"* would never have had room to thrive in better days. *The Mill on the Floss* would have been called "The Mill on the Floss; a tale founded upon fact. Being a Romance delineating contemporary Manners, from the pen of a Maiden Lady"; and there would have been a dedication and, I hope, a motto as well.

I confess I am all for mottoes, by the way; not written round rooms, where they tend to swarm and breed and get out of hand, but put in pretty little miniature print on a title-page, preferably in Greek, in Latin, or even in English. In French also (so that it be of the Eighteenth Century); but not in a language unknown to the run of the cultivated, such as Hebrew, Tamil, or Arabic, for that is an affectation. A motto, moreover, is best when it tells the reader something new, and also gives him something to think about; and the one I like best is one I have written myself, and quoted perhaps three hundred times. Let me quote it here again for the three hundred and first:

This is a book which those who take it up will not readily lay down, and those who lay it down will not readily take up.

Instead of mottoes nowadays we have the publisher's puff outside, which is nearly always exaggerated and makes one think of an advertisement for pills; but then, for that matter, I deplore all dust covers *en bloc*. It is to dust covers that we owe this offensive trick.

To return, then, to lengthy titles. How much better it would have been for the time just past, the last quarter of the Nineteenth Century and the first years of the Twentieth, if people had always quoted Darwin's great work under its true and lengthy title, instead of by an abbreviated one; for that famous book is not called, as you might imagine from so much repetition, *The Origin of the Species*; it is called "The Origin of Species, by means of Natural Selection, or the Preservation of Favoured Races in the Struggle for Life." There you have a proper exposition of what is to follow. You sit down to read a piece of argument which profoundly affected the thought of its time, and bade fair, for a full generation, to fix the philosophy of the future. Anyone can write on the origin of the species. The stupidest and the dullest and the emptiest book might bear the title; so might the most startlingly foolish, as might be a book by the Fundamentalists (pretty name for a pretty thing), or a disquisition to prove that there were no such things as species at all; that every form merged into every other—which would be still worse than Fundamentalism; or even a disquisition to prove that the idea of A Species, as it was a general idea, had no real existence—which piece of nonsense, being plumb

Nominalism (forgive me!), would be the very nadir or last word of stupidity. But Darwin's title with that determining clause of *Natural Selection*, the only original thing in his book and the whole purport of it, tells you what you are going to read, sets your limits, directs your mind, prepares you for the great business to which you are coming and to the exposition of which he devoted his life, and so wasted it; since he has been proved wrong. There is this other excellence in the long title, that it has rhythm; it is, as it were, the brother to the line or phrase, or to the couplet, which may be called the smallest complete form of full human expression.

Very short phrases, and therefore titles, are admirable as jests or masterpieces of trick, but they are not, and cannot be, complete. For instance, suppose a man calls his book "Vale" (I have no real book in my mind). That may mean "Farewell"; or it may mean a depression in the landscape; or it may be the hero's name. Whatever it means, you cannot find out until you have read on a bit; whereas the object of a title is to direct you to reading by telling you more or less what you are to read. And even if you guess the title right, and find it means "Farewell," as you expected, you do not know farewell to what, nor why, nor anything about it. But if it were called "Vale: Being an Old Man's Farewell to this World, with his Retrospection upon a long and, as he hopes, well-spent Life in the Cure of Souls, with a Preface by the Honourable Charles Gowlthorpe," and so on, you might well grow excited at the prospect of a really juicy piece of autobiography; for you must know very little of English letters if you have not discovered that diaries and the like, written down in an

English parsonage, have produced, in proportion to their amount, a greater number of good books than any other sort (I hasten to add that this is not true of sermons). Witness the *Vicar of Morwenstow*, White's *Selborne*, and, as a parallel or by extension to fiction, *The Vicar of Wakefield.*

Consider the *Encyclopædia Britannica*, and how its superscription might have been embellished and developed. I do not complain of it too much. The word *Britannica* tells one a good deal, and the date of its first edition enables anyone of sufficient instruction to know it for what it is: something of a counterblast to the Frenchmen who had set the ball rolling. But how much better if the earlier edition had borne beneath the first words the continuation: "Being a series of Disjointed Essays dealing at length upon a great quantity of subjects, Theological, Geological, Biological, Ontological, Illogical, and -ogical of every kind. The whole sturdily stuffed with a puissant national spirit and paying little attention to the vagaries of dirty foreigners, save, indeed, where these were noble Germans; the historical, especially, being designed to make the reader feel comfortable and to nourish him with pleasant illusions." I say this of the earlier edition of that mighty work, which can be put to so very many uses, from keeping the door open to playing an unending game of spotting errors. Here length of title would have been of advantage and profit, and still more of delight. Then, to the latest edition one might have put something very different: "Being a Revision of the old Back Number, gingered up; with a due appreciation of the part to be played from the word 'Now' by God's own Country.

127

Do you take me? Liable to lead to very violent protest by the stuffed but made for peeled eyes, and with no mercy on boneheads. All manner of illustration, mainly from our side." If there had been a title like that stuck boldly on to the front page, we should not have had the deplorable quarrels which have saddened us all.

I forbear to suggest a new and lengthier title for the Bible, lest I offend—though I can imagine a magnificent half-page suitable for modern ears—but I do warmly advise some elaboration of the far too curt word "Bradshaw." There are infinite possibilities here, and though no one would take advantage of my suggestion in print, you might do worse than pass a wet afternoon composing a good elaboration and dedication for the same, and finding a motto. I suggest: "The train of Venus did outshine them all."

★ XXIII ★

On Jonathan Swift

A SOLID piece of comfort in the times through which we have to live is the permanence of Swift. He alone of the great prose masters survives on one level, in spite of hostile or indifferent or enthusiastic mood; and that although our literary moods have fallen into chaos.

There is no writer of English for whom modern England should be less sympathetic; and (save in his case) it would seem that grave modern lack of sympathy, though it does not kill the reputation of a name, kills the reading of that to which the famous name was signed.

Pope is an example. It may be fairly said that for one who reads Pope to-day among educated men, there were fifty in Pope's own day. Swift should be far less sympathetic than Pope. He was essentially a satirist, and the modern reader does not only fail to understand satire, but withdraws from it as from an unpleasant experience. He is not only bewildered by it; he actually dislikes it. Again, that which Swift satirised has passed. It is no good pointing out that a man who exposes the vileness of human nature has an eternal theme. In the concrete the things he made fools of are no longer known. For instance, his chief butt is the courtier, because in his day a simulation of power still attached to monarchy, and it was not even certain that monarchy might not return. To-day the courtier has disappeared. The politician has taken his place; and all the anger of Swift against the courtier is anger against what is to us a void, and all his indignation against the courtier is wasted effort. Yet his satire on the dead courtier survives, and suggests what we might write to-day (had we a Swift) upon the moribund Parliamentary Politician.

Again, Swift is perpetually harping on Ireland. He was born in Ireland; and may be called spiritually, through all the middle and later part of his life, a sort of "native but naturalised" Irishman. Now, of Ireland our readers of to-day may properly be said to know nothing. They know less of the place and temper than they do of those of France, let alone Italy, which many of us do half-understand. Yet his writing upon that foreign country, and in the air of that foreign country, actively survives.

Nor is this all. The very Ireland with which he is concerned and which he takes for granted, alien to the reader because it is Ireland, is doubly alien because his was a phase of Irish history which has melted into nothingness. Swift wrote for and about and to a governing alien minority. In his eyes the mass of the Irish are submerged (presumably) for ever. The Dublin which we find in Swift is a Dublin of his Protestant co-religionists, and down to the street hawkers and up to the bishops it is of, for, and to a Protestant world that he writes. One may fairly say that nothing else exists for him in his surroundings, save as a very vague background or mass which can never actively count or be vocal again. Put Swift into Catholic Ireland to-day, and he might think himself in another planet—especially in Dublin. Yet what he has to say is of the same power as it was when he was saying it more than two hundred years ago.

It is perhaps still more remarkable that he survives in spite of iconoclasm. He survives in spite of his ceaseless onslaught upon that which is for us an idol. Whether we know it or not, all our history and three-quarters of our literature is Whig. Its heroes are Whig heroes; its villains are those whom Whiggery made out to be villains. Swift's whole temper is anti-Whig, and, though he changed masters, his best work was done against that political theory, against its exponents and its beneficiaries. I can read unendingly, and I hope many others can and do, *The Public Spirit of the Whigs*. A modern writer who should to-day so thrust himself against what had become the fixed historical tradition of the country would be neglected for a crank. Swift is accepted.

Now, why does the great master so survive? Let us begin with a few negatives. It is not because he wrote one immensely popular book which can be bowdlerised for children, and enjoy the immortality which a good child's book enjoys from generation to generation. If Swift had never written of giants and of dwarfs, he would be just as famous, and would perhaps be read to-day as much as he is. He is certain of a strong reading public for the future indefinitely.

Obviously, this is not because he conforms to any national doctrine of our time. Thus the great modern doctrine of the impeccability of lawyers which sceptics have assailed but which still has great strength, was not so much as conceivable to Swift. He writes of the legal profession as one might write of poisoning, and of lawyers as of base scoundrels. His attachment to dogmatic religion is equally alien to us, and his contempt for that sort of free thought which is everywhere in our drawing-rooms. He defends the creed, and he defends it with that intellectual scepticism which is in the unintelligence of to-day almost forgotten.

Nor does his strength lie in the national talent for portrait painting. There is no "character" in all Swift. Even in the immortal *Tale of a Tub* Lord Peter himself is hardly a living person, and his two brothers are still less individual. In such a lack of power to portray the individual, Swift is unique. The whole flood of English letters, from a century before his time right down to our own, is a crowd of living men. In Swift there is not one. Why, then, is the position of Swift unchanging?

I think I should say, in answer to this question, that the chief cause of Swift's immovability is Style. The word is abused; but rightly used it is significant. Swift excelled in, he survives by, style in prose.

It was one of the most just among the many just pronouncements of Lord Chesterfield, in his *Letters to His Son*, that Swift should be taken as the model of English prose. For hardness, sufficiency and exactitude he has no peer and no rival. His prose is without the least suspicion of rhetoric, and its rhythms are so broken, and at the same time so concealed, that I doubt if he was himself aware of them. On nine pages out of ten they cannot be analysed at all. But since prose style is excellent in proportion as it is lucid, Swift is first. There never was a man who could say what he had to say more clearly, nor with a better certitude that every reader of every class would immediately understand him.

It is strange that this virtue is apparent in the same degree with the first of his sentences and with the last: stranger because the end of Jonathan Swift, as he himself prophesied, was a tragic mental decay. Now when madness or imbecility is the nature of a writer's exit from this world (and such an exit is a frequent penalty exacted by the dreadful trade of letters), we expect, and commonly we find, as the years advance, an inclination to confusion. It was so with Pascal, whose exit was of that kind. I think we may admit that it was in some degree true of Ruskin. There is no trace of it in Swift. He writes up to the end as sharply and with as hard an edge as in his early manhood—and during the tragic years he writes no more.

It is to be noted that in this admirable prose there are no mannerisms; and that in itself helps to account for the similarity of it in each lustre of his writing life. For it is the mark of age that a writer's mannerisms, if he has any (and nearly all writers have), increase upon him. A mannerism is a vehicle; it saves effort both in thought and in construction; it is commonly praised by flatterers who are the guides of writers as they grow old. Also mannerisms are a label by which the man who desires reputation knows that he can be recognised. Further, they ensure a public; for the public, having grown used to expect a mannerism, is satisfied on finding it again. Swift has not such a thing as a mannerism about him. And yet if anyone present you with a short paragraph of his you will know it at once for Swift's. No one else wrote like that. No one since Swift has written like that. No one before Swift wrote like that.

And there is this last thing to be said about him (which is true of so very few), that his writing never grows old. Young men not yet born will read it, as I read it when it broke upon me in a wealth of delight more than forty years ago. The generations will recognise and salute it in turn, as I do now. For, to tell you the truth, I finished *The Public Spirit of the Whigs* only a fortnight ago, it being perhaps my twentieth or my hundredth reading of it. And I am now setting off home to read it again.

On Thinking

CANON DIMNET of Cambrai lately wrote a little book upon the *Art of Thinking*. He wrote it, I believe, in the English tongue; but whether it be a translation or from his own pen (which is the more likely, for he writes English like an Englishman), it is a book without the mark of a foreign origin; and perhaps he chose English for his medium on the consideration that thinking had often been condemned during the last century and even lately in the English tongue as a solvent of judgment and instinctive power. I desire to take the title of this book for a text, and to affirm that the business of Thinking has been somewhat under-estimated of late: I desire to proclaim its modest value: to urge its use (in moderation, of course), and to say, even though I must say it timidly, a word in its favour. Come, let me take up the unpopular side, play the devil's advocate, and write a cautious brief in defence of this half-forgotten exercise, Thinking.

It was said some months ago by a witty Englishman, in praise of his own people, on returning from some foreign conference or other, that there was written up in

flaming red letters upon the cliffs of Dover, for all
returning men to read:

Thou shalt not Think. Thought is the foe of action.
Therefore by Thinking men and nations perish.

It is a precept which has been repeated in various
forms a thousand times. I doubt its soundness. It still
seems to me that Thinking must have some good about
it, and that those who decry Thinking are misled by an
abuse of terms: an ambiguity. For the word "thinking"
is used of musing, as when we say of a man run over
by a motor car that he was plunged in thought: and it
is used of doubt, as when one says: "I don't think the
earth is flat: I know it"; it is used of vain illusion, as of
Algernon, who thought himself the hell of a fellow; but
it should more properly be used of discernment, so that
by thought we see clearly the consequence of things, and
by intelligence decide affairs and reach success in
conclusions.

I have noticed not infrequently upon my rambles
through this world that men (my brethren and similars)
would order animals about: great strong animals, such
as horned beeves, fierce dogs, and nervous horses; and
that they were able so to do (it seemed to me) was due
to their superior power of Thought. Observing this
result, I have ever felt a certain anxiety lest, if we give
up Thinking altogether, we may not become the prey
of other nations more exercised in the practice.

Then, also, I have noticed that fame (which we all
desire) is not unattached to this art of Thinking. Of
close and clear thinkers there occur to me—Euclid,

136

Descartes, Aquinas, even Cicero, and no one can say that they will be easily forgotten. Newton, by the way, should be added, and Locke, and John Stuart Mill; three prominent men who seem to have rebelled against the patriotic order emblazoned upon the cliffs of Dover. But, talking of patriotism, there have been other rebels. For instance, not only was political economy founded here in England, where we are told no man should be allowed to Think, but the inferences and deductions of geology as well; for the beginnings of Geology are English. Then there is the whole science and practice of the Law, wherein I admit men will continually protest they prefer good honest sense to thinking, but wherein also I notice there is quite a lot of Thinking done, sometimes a little too finely.

Then there are all those of the delicate professions, if I may use that term. I mean, the careers in which men advance by a certain light dexterity in appreciation of others and by the laying of subtle plans. Such are promoters, share-shufflers, big-business men, money dealers, sharpers, those of the three-card trick and the great army of snatchers and lifters. Which of them would survive if he did not think—rapidly, clearly, continually?

When, therefore, I hear the phrase that what is of importance to mortals is character, not intellect, I am so moved that I fall into verse—a thing habitual with versifiers when their emotions are stirred—and on this very matter have I composed a short epic, the first lines of which I will now humbly put before you, reminding you, however, that they are copyright, and reserving the sequel that I may sell it again later:

137

I knew a man who used to say
(Not once, but twenty times a day)
That in the turmoil and the strife—
His very phrase—of human life,
The thing of ultimate effect
Was character: not intellect.
He therefore was at constant pains
To atrophy his puny brains,
And registered success in this
Beyond the dreams of avarice.

The epic goes on to describe his career, how, when he had become completely imbecile, he was selected for the highest posts in the land, and died—for even such men must die at last—saturated with glory, rolling in money and a model for all of us.

But this poem, I must warn you, was by way of satire, or something the opposite of what it plainly states. It was malicious. It was not to be taken literally, for within my own great soul I knew well that some measure of intellect was essential, even to public life, let alone to the running of a whelk stall.

I fancy that those who decry the ancient and honourable practice of Thinking are mixing it up with two things very different, which are called Deduction from Insufficient Premises, and Deduction from False Premises; or perhaps they are mixing it up with Argufying—which of all the detestable habits of man is perhaps the most intolerable—unless, indeed, it be set to work upon matters wholly undiscoverable, wherein it is a very tolerable pastime. Indeed, you may note that men in their cups generally talk metaphysics. And this, let me tell you, is not particularly true of the overeducated, but of all men whatsoever. It was but the other day I heard two men, with no pretence to any excess of culture, shouting at each other in the bar of an inn close against the shores of the Southern Sea, and one of them kept on saying, "How d'you know that what you saw *was* Bill's ketch, anyhow?" And the other kept on replying, "Why, it stands to reason that if I saw the thing it was there." Wherein was developed all the quarrel of Kant and the sceptics with the peripatetics, and of sophists with common sense from the beginning of time; also the dear little fuss about phenomena.

And as for Thinking interfering with action, that is using one word in two senses. It is not Thinking that interferes with action; Thinking decides action. It is hesitation in Thought that interferes with action; it is paralysis in Thought that interferes with action, like that weariness of the mind wherein a tune goes on buzzing in one's head. The man who keeps on saying, "Shall I? Shall I not?" is not Thinking, he is cutting the nerve of Thought. And even if Thinking have no practical value (though I stoutly maintain it has), at the least it is an absorbing exercise, bridging over those empty moments when we have neither scandal to talk against our neighbours, nor money to filch from them, nor vapid books to read.

Therefore do I think that I shall continue to think; and whether you think I think right in so thinking I care not, for I think so.

★ XXV ★

The Great Minister

I HAVE had occasion of late to read a great deal upon the subject of two men, William Cecil, Lord Burghley, and Armand du Plessis, Cardinal Richelieu. The better to understand them, I have read a little—but not nearly enough—upon the third of the trinity, Bismarck. As I did so, I continually asked myself, what was the nature of their achievement? What factors went to create that resultant? For this was my motive in seeking the evidence.

I was attempting to discover what made for success in a particular type, which may most accurately be called "the Great Minister." To-day we no longer have that type before us. The conditions under which it grew up and acted are no longer present. We still use the term "minister," but in a different sense. The qualities which make a man successful as a Minister under a parliamentary system, or which make him a dictator under a nominal republic or under a nominal royal power, are quite different from those which made the Great Minister of old.

The Great Minister of European history, throughout centuries of its development, but particularly between the Renaissance and our own time, was not the master of the Crown, government or country which he served, as are the modern dictators; nor was he one of many compeers in a profession of politics. He was the right-hand man, but also the supreme agent and lieutenant of a real master.

He was something more than an agent. He was that through whom the legal authority acted, and, in the height of his power, was identified with such authority. The Great Minister could not have come into existence without a fixed moral authority which he served and which was hereditary, elective, conventional—but, at any rate, not dependent upon any form of ability and therefore needing aid.

The Great Minister could not come into existence in one of those very rare phenomena, the aristocratic states, because, though he was only a lieutenant, his rule was pretty nearly a one-man rule, and one-man rule is a thing no aristocratic state will tolerate. He came into existence as something necessary to governments which were sincerely regarded by the governed as being at once legitimate, all-powerful, and vested in particular personalities. Whatever may have been the realities of the situation, the mass of Englishmen in the second half of the sixteenth century thought of the monarch as being personally all-powerful. So did the mass of Frenchmen in the early seventeenth century. Cecil therefore, and Richelieu after him, could only act in the name of and by the authority of the Crown. Yet each in fact governed.

It would have been impossible for Elizabeth to have got rid of Cecil, only difficult for Louis XIII to have got rid of Richelieu; and when Macaulay said that there was no room in one government for an Elizabeth and a Richelieu, he was, as usual, quite unhistorical. There was far more personal power vested in Louis XIII than ever there was in Elizabeth. But both men had to act in the name, and with the moral support of the Crown; because society around them thought in terms of the Crown.

Under such conditions the first of the qualities which made them was *range*. Each had that very rare capacity for grasping a great mass of detail in a number of very different fields, which rare capacity goes to the making of men in any profession dealing with general activities. It is invariably present in the great strategists and in the great diplomatists. It is founded in part upon the base function of memory, but much more on the vividness of imagination, by which a man actually sees all the details at work and follows them as he would follow various and distinctively clothed individuals. How rare that quality is, the quality of dealing with very many things *of many different kinds*, all at once and abreast, you may test by its converse: the ease with which you can get a simple order obeyed, the difficulty with which you will get a complex one obeyed.

The second quality which went to make the Great Minister was a sense of proportion, which includes a judgment of the exact moment in which an action may be undertaken. This is a commoner quality than the first, or, rather, it is a quality more delicately graded than the first. You pass quickly from the man who may attend to a reasonable number of details to the man who can attend to a host of them. And you pass with violence from the ordinary man who can only attend to one kind of thing, to the very exceptional man who can attend to five or six kinds. But in matters of proportion, or judgment, you get a great number of the superior sort who judge well enough, and the difference between these and those who are nearly always right is not startling. Also, there is an element of luck with the most successful. I will give two examples.

Elizabeth ordered the Spanish treasure at Plymouth and Southampton to be returned to its rightful owners. Within twenty-four hours Cecil had brushed her aside and ordered its detainment. He was running a very great risk, for the last thing he wanted was war; but he judged he could do it without war, and so cripple an ally—and he proved right. Richelieu determined to force the Pass at Susa. If he had failed, he would have been in a much worse position than before. He succeeded; and it was all over in a few minutes.

Again, Cecil, at the very origin of the reign, risked the keeping out of the Papal Nuncio by making one violent scene, in which, as usual, he overrode the Queen. Had he failed so early in the business, his whole plan would have crashed. He succeeded. Richelieu risked the execution of Montmorency. It was going to the extreme limits of his power; it seemed as though he might be going just beyond those limits. He succeeded.

No one can say how much in these two gambles was luck, and how much vision—or rather, how much the exact weighing of chances.

But the third and most remarkable factor in the making of these Great Ministers of the past was industry; and it is here that you get the chief difference between them and the official or politician acting under other conditions.

The official, military or civil, is, save in exceptional moments of turbulence, dependent upon seniority. A minimum of industry is demanded of him. By which I do not mean that officials are not industrious, but that only a certain fixed and known amount of work is necessary to their career. Politicians have no use for industry at all. I could quote a dozen who have made large fortunes without work: at the cost of no more than occasional blackmail or taking bribes. The politician depends upon I know not what, but certainly not upon industry.

Now the quality of industry in the Great Minister, serving, and substituted for, a real master, was at once unique and supreme. It was unique because he was exercising it in a world where no one else would dream of exercising it. He was among favourites and courtiers, adventurers, people counting on their birth, a mass of apparent competitors who were not really competing with him because each was thinking of brilliant appearance, or excitement, and personal pleasures, or the silly ambition of being called a favourite. In such a world it was almost impossible for any man to work really hard. And the one man who *did* work hard went through it like iron through mud. When Dudley wanted to despoil Seymour he turned at once to Cecil, as much as to say, "What is your price for selling your master?" And Cecil sold his master; it was the turn in his fortunes. But why did Dudley turn to Cecil? Because Cecil alone had worked; Cecil alone had all the letters docketed and filed and endorsed, and, stored in his memory, the

144

reports of spies, and, already provided for in his imagination, the possibility of such a sudden opportunity. Only one man of the gang was really working: Cecil.

When Louis XIII was in doubt about the last intrigues of his mother, the man who had sat up all night collating documents, checking the reports, and weighing the credibility of evidence, was Richelieu. It was no use asking the opinion of half a dozen other people, as one might to-day the opinion of this politician who had spent a week-end at Bunting Towers, and that other who had spent a week-end at Le Touquet, or that other who had spent it in bed; there was only one man really working: Richelieu.

I would go so far as to say that this quality of cumulative industry is even rarer than that of range. Many a man works hard at a hobby or a habit that interests him. Many a man can force himself to work from a sense of duty or from necessity. But to work as with gluttony along those lines which one's station in life appears to close for one, *that* is extraordinary. Those who observe this rare phenomenon among contemporaries commonly ask, "How do they find time for it?" The only answer I know is that they work at a much higher voltage than other men: they master a map or a page of writing while another man would still be trying to grasp a paragraph, or beginning to make out the scale on which the map was drawn.

And the last element, of course, is luck—and especially the luck of living.

William Cecil did not control the weather at the end of July 1588. Richelieu did not prevent Marie de Médicis from bolting the door of the servants' passage

145

in the Luxembourg; her own impetuosity and not his intrigue was to blame. For the matter of that, Cecil might have choked on a fish-bone during any of the six Lents or the several hundred abstinence days under Mary Tudor, during which he was so fervent a Catholic; or Richelieu might have died during any one of those mad foamings at the mouth when he imagined that he had been turned into a horse. Contrariwise, each died full of years and honours (as the honour of this world goes and as the years of that time went). Poor Bismarck outlived his activity; but that has in no way diminished his fame, nor the magnitude of his achievements.

Will such Great Ministers come again? I think so. But if I were asked how, I should reply, "By way of the Dictators." Dictatorship in maturity brings forth Kingship: Kingship, servants of this kind. But if you differ from me, I can give you a very good arbiter between us, to wit, any reasonably well-educated man who shall happen to be living and observing the world in the year 2073.

XXVI

Henry V

I READ the other day that the hilt and blade of Henry V's conquering sword, preserved at Westminster, had been more fully identified through some manuscript or other. Perhaps they will be shown in the future alongside with his saddle and his shield. He would have liked that. He was a great soldier.

It is true of all men, public or private, that their real selves are different from their labels and their legends; that is inevitable. It is especially true of national heroes. It is more especially true of such few among the national heroes of the English as died before the prodigious moral revolution of the later sixteenth and earlier seventeenth centuries had transformed the country. Henry V has suffered (or enjoyed) this contrast between reality and myth more than any other figure I can recall out of the English Middle Ages.

There are many reasons for this. He came at a moment when the language of the upper class was gradually changing from French to what to-day is English. He came of a cadet branch which had violently usurped the Throne by revolution and murder, and which, none the less, was able to transmit its own legend through the Tudors and to establish a sort of Lancastrian official version of that century wherein the ancient England perished. He was a great warrior and a successful warrior, dying at the height of his success; and a great warrior and a successful warrior at a moment when the new religion of nationalism was beginning to pierce through the old religion of Christendom.

He had the good fortune to fire the imagination of William Shakespeare, and so to rise from the dead in a personality very different from his own, much simpler, immensely more popular.

To all this I would add another point deriving from the one I have just mentioned. I have said that he had the luck to die at the height of his military success. Now, from this there derived, necessarily, an exalted legend concerning him. Think what Napoleon would be to the French if he had died before the Russian expedition, and if the subsequent failures were attached to the names of apparently incompetent successors! Such was Henry V's admirable fate. In many a tavern of England, during the thirties and early forties of the fifteenth century, men scarred from the French wars told the deeds they could remember in their youth under such a captain, and cursed the bunglers who (in some way they did not understand) were throwing away the fruits of the earlier reign. I fancy it was from such a tradition, long preserved, that the spectacular figure, presented to the world one hundred and fifty years later on the stage, owed its eminence.

What was he? He was spare, diseased, indomitable; with a very sharp, prominent profile, narrow head, cold but keen eyes; possessed of two qualities which formed his whole story—a very high military aptitude and an isolated will. These qualities were supported by other qualities less rare; he could appreciate a political situation, domestic or foreign; he could determine its larger lines; he could frame a policy suitable to each. It is probable that had he lived he could have carried out such policies in full, at home and abroad.

What then? Then we should have had a dominating Western realm from the Scotch border to the Mediterranean, with its capital in Paris, weighing as much as the Empire, or more, deciding the fate of the Church during the great quarrel between the Councils and the Papacy, and presumably affecting the development of Spain. The centre of gravity of the whole West would have lain in Northern France, and there would have been reconstituted a Diocese of the Gauls.

He did not live. He died of his insufficient body; its dissolution hastened by, burnt out with campaigning and intense planning and intriguing. He was barely thirty-five when he so died in that old stonework dungeon of Vincennes; and, dying, he knew (it must have been an agony for him to know) that he could only leave instructions which might be bungled, lacking his personal command.

He was filled with religion, but religion of a twisted kind. When he rode into Paris down the rue St. Martin, the Roman road through the city (reversing Cæsar's order), when he kissed all the way the relics which the priests held up to him, it was no mere show. He was fervent in these things; and the whole world knows how he whispered, as he died, that his soul had hungered to retake Jerusalem. It is rhetorical but not unjust to say that he was, in spirit, the last of the Crusading kings. He was abominably cruel. He said that war without burning was like beef without mustard. He added fuel to what needed no addition—the strict and organised repression of heresy in the crisis which ended with the disruption of Christendom. It is true that the Church in England had fallen into the hands of those great lords who cared first for their revenues and very much less for doctrine. It is true that the Lancastrian usurpation needed to rely upon such Lords Ecclesiastical, as it needed to rely upon their brothers and cousins, the Lords Temporal. But we must not read into that truth the repeated falsehood that the Lancastrians only used the Church by way of policy. They were intense in their worship, and no one of them more than this one, the greatest of them.

Henry V came as a lad into an inheritance which he must have known to be most unsafe. Its instability spurred him to the famous effort he made. His father (that broad-faced, russet-bearded man, foredoomed to death from a taint in blood, but at the moment of his crime still vigorous) had ousted his cousin Richard with the vilest forms of treason, hypocrisy and lying, and then—surely without doubt—had murdered him. To the men of his own time, and (as I believe) to Henry IV's own soul, it was an abomination. The popular conscience judged the thing aright, and the criminal himself was haunted by the necessity for expiation. The story, doubtful or true (perhaps disproved but still arguable), that this king's body was thrown overboard by the sailors taking it down the Thames in their terror lest it should bring shipwreck, is at any rate symbolic of how Henry IV was looked upon by the common people. Now, his son may have argued that, with Richard dead, and no male heir of the Plantagenet blood surviving with better right than his own, the evil had been conjured. Even so the foreign war was undertaken by that young man (though by advice) with the desire to make his line founded and secure.

Having undertaken the adventure, with what genius does he not complete it! There is, of course, a major element of chance in all military affairs; but mark his way of accepting gratefully every favour which Fortune gave him and in mastering her when she teased him with obstacles. I think she, being a woman, must have loved him before the end.

He marched out from Harfleur with something less than a division—11,000 men. It was his business to get to Calais immediately, by rapid marches. In his eyes it must have seemed not only his business but a necessity. He found the passages of the Somme blocked; first the lower fords, then bridge after bridge. He still marched up stream. What qualities there must have been in that young commander (he was but twenty-eight) to keep discipline and even enthusiasm alive within the little army; to carry them on, covering more than fifteen miles a day, across the great bend of the river, determined to force a passage somewhere, even if he had to turn the obstacle by getting right down south and round across the shallow sources of the stream—with Calais (to which his back was turned) his objective all the time! What a handling of men to preserve that force without serious losses in days when common provision failed and they were gathering nuts for sustenance!

They turned northward, not challenging the walled towns: they heard of the great host gathered against them beyond the crossing of the Ternoise. They went up on the October evening, through the drenched fields, to the huts and tall trees of Maisoncelles. They slept in what barns they could or bivouacked in the rain. The next dull autumn dawn was Agincourt.

Agincourt did not give him that Anglo-French realm which had been the dream of the Plantagenets, inherited from the House of Normandy for now more than three hundred years. If he came at last to plucking the fruit (which rotted after his death) it was not directly through that Picard victory, but by a masterly diplomatic play between the warring factions of the Capetian House. Here again fate helped him; but how admirably he seized opportunity!

And all this done, he died. And the folly of others and the turn of fate, and the intervention of revelation, of vision and of whatever accompanies the Higher Powers undid it all.

The Maid rode over it: against that riding no mere mortal could make calculation.

Yet even as he died, murmuring of the Holy City, Henry must have known what a tangle he left, though he could not have known how the undoing of his effort would come. It is very often so with those who achieve much. They cannot but foresee that their achievement will fail at last, but they cannot conceive by what unexpected agency it will fail; they only know that nothing men plan is fully and finally performed.

XXVII

La Rochelle

LA ROCHELLE differs from what may be called the "fossil towns" of Europe in that the period which it fossilises appeals to few. The physical aspect of La Rochelle is not what the nineteenth-century tourist looked for when he sought the picturesque. It is not of the Middle Ages. It is not the model or mausoleum of any period of architecture with which the traveller was enamoured when travel began to be a search for antiquity. There are things very picturesque about it, and one or two things mediæval; but the particular quality of La Rochelle is that it has been fixed as by a spell just at that moment in its history when it was most famous, just at that moment after which its importance to European society disappeared.

Save that the walls have been pulled down (and a great pity it is *to us* that they should ever have been destroyed), it is a city of the first half of the seventeenth century; a city of the time when the violent religious quarrel in France and in Europe was as yet undecided, of the time when every town could stand a siege; of a time when even isolated castles still survived, and were only in process of disappearing before the artillery of the various princes and governments.

La Rochelle is like an etching by Colot. There you have the towers of the Gothic planted here and there, the arcaded streets, the odd remnants of the Renaissance in corners, the steep slate roofs which are associated in the French mind with the name of Louis XIII. But the traveller filled with historical fiction (or, I suppose, to-day, with quasi-historical films) will not feel antiquity in La Rochelle. He will not recognise, as he will in Nuremberg, one period, or at Aiguesmortes another, or at Old Carcassonne another, or in the Place des Vosges in Paris yet another.

That is the whole point of the place. Because it is really of one period, it does not seem to be of one period. At any moment of history, in any town which has not laid itself out for being a museum or a show, you have a mixture of the various ages, yet over it all at any one moment the spirit of that moment.

If you could halt the process of time, for instance, in Westminster to-day, and leave Westminster as it is for three hundred years more, the people of three hundred years hence would not say, "This is of the Middle Ages," though the Abbey is its principal building. They would not say, "This is of the mid-Victorian false effort," though the mid-Victorian false effort runs riot all around from the excessive bulk of the Houses of Parliament to the statues in Parliament Square, and to the more dignified imitation of Italian in the Government buildings. They would not say, "This is of the seventeenth century," though there they have before them two of the noblest and most characteristic examples of England in the seventeenth century, Whitehall and the admirable reproduction of Inigo Jones's design (as I have been told it is) in the oval of the Education Office. They would not say it was Georgian, in spite of the Guildhall. No; the observer would say, if he were learned enough to know his business, "Here is what a part of London looked like in the first half of the twentieth century."

Now that is exactly what you have in La Rochelle. La Rochelle is 1620-1650, left standing, caught, as it were, in the day when men only preserved mediæval things because it was too expensive to pull them down, or because they still had some direct use; in the day when men destroyed the loveliest of the Gothic without scruple, mainly from religious hatreds; in the day when the most ponderous dull efforts of the "false good taste" were burdening Europe with unornamented stone.

The degree in which La Rochelle is thus caught, like a fly in amber, presenting exactly this period and no other, is a degree, I think, unique. Let me give some examples of it.

The harbour is of the same size as it was when Denbigh tried to force his way in, when the envoys of Buckingham sailed between its towers to hearten the townsfolk, when the great siege starved them into surrender. It has silted a good deal deeper in mud than it was in those days (it does not pay anyone to dredge it, for it has been superseded by new work along the coast). Perhaps the mud flats outside show a little higher above low tide than they did three hundred years ago (though I don't think that here there is much difference). Otherwise it is the same place—the same narrow fairway going down with a racing ebb upon it between the shoals towards the open sea; the great mole which Richelieu had built to starve out the city and cut it off from succour is still apparent at low water; his tower on it at the centre, and even the site of the principal royal work, "Fort Louis," can be traced on the present sports-ground—the line of its earthworks still remains.

The gaunt Cathedral imposes the will of royalty upon its rebellious Huguenot town, as it did in the days when it rose upon the ruins of the lovely mediæval thing which the Huguenots had—after their wont—destroyed.

Even Guiton is still there; Guiton the little, broad-shouldered, stocky man whose heroism should be legendary throughout Europe, and is perhaps sufficiently famous with a sufficient number to save his name for remote posterity. He was the genius of the defence. There mingled in his spirit the intense energy of the Calvinist offensive, the intense local patriotism of the merchant city. Guiton is, you may say, the very siege of La Rochelle itself; and his statue in front of the beautiful little Renaissance Town Hall is alive. It almost moves. You cannot forget the man when you have left it and walk about his streets.

Providence, or the Dæmon of History, has seen to it that this preservation of La Rochelle should continue, for there has been no temptation to increase or to improve the port, or to enlarge the boundaries of the city. Out upon the Atlantic, facing the Island of Rhé where Buckingham fought so well and failed, our time has created a vast new series of works, which are those of La Pallice. It is not yet completed; it is already formidable, though it still looks rather like a workshop than a town. There you may see the great docks for the submarines, and the repairing sheds, and the warehouses, springing up; and the big new sea wall, and the great sandy spaces allotted and rapidly filling with buildings.

For the first time in my life, I think, I was grateful to modern ugliness, when I considered that it would be the salvation of La Rochelle. For unless La Pallice should grow eastward so much out of measure as to encroach on the old town, its neighbour, still separated from it by some miles, La Pallice will act as a screen for La Rochelle, or as a lightning conductor. The Atlantic liners which already touch there will have their hotels on the spot (perhaps they have one already), the modern port city will be completed and La Rochelle will be left in peace. So be it.

I wish the French spirit would allow (which it will not) a religious census. After all, if it did, people would at once rebel against it, and it would be of no use. Let me rather say that I wish some power were present in the town to tell you how much of the old Huguenot spirit remains, and whether I am just or fanciful when I feel, as I do when I walk its mournful streets, the spirits of the great siege all around me.

About the city inland lie the marshy flats which one is tempted to call eternal, even in the changing modern world—for who will ever build on such? The mournful empty horizons are the same, and the sea birds complaining.

★ XXVIII ★

The Divine Bottle

I TREMBLE as I write that title down! Another has used the phrase before me, but he has been dead these four hundred years, or near, and times have changed. My dread is lest the title and the theme be what politicians and sub-editors call controversial. I have never quite mastered the meaning of that last word, but I know that it is something abominable and to be shunned. And here let me repeat an old story which was told me by and of a friend of mine. You have heard it often, so it will approach you with the grace of familiar things. In my own poor *corpus* of letters it has cropped up, I fancy, a dozen times. But no matter. Here goes.

This friend of mine was asked to give what is called "an address," not in the sense in which you give such things to the officers of the law, but in the sense in which you give such things to the evening audiences of the suburbs. No subject had been given out, but just as he got up to speak his chairman whispered to him that he was requested not to touch upon politics or religion, as these were controversial. Whereupon did this friend of mine, standing his full height and speaking out strongly, like Hector before the trenches round the ships (I hope it was Hector), trumpet these memorable words:

"I have been asked not to speak upon politics or religion; and since these two subjects comprise all that is of interest to the human race, I will sit down again."

Such was his address—worthy to be engraved on bronze and set up in the market place: a speech more true and more informing than any that have been made since the death of Oratory, in Florence.

I say, then, that I tremble; but having begun, I must go on. As Napoleon said, using mixed metaphors, to his Marshal by night in Moscow, when it was decided to march southward upon Maloyaroslavets, instead of towards St. Petersburg, "It is the counsel of the Lion; but now the wine is drawn, we must drink it." Yet lions drink no wine—which brings me back to wine, and to my fear lest I offend.

For it may be that there is an anti-wine religion going about, and that to praise wine, or even to talk about it, is to inflict a grievous wound on some rich man or woman perhaps in Parliament—a thing I would rather die than do. Those who may be attached to this anti-wine religion will not bear anything in praise of wine, and will also, I suppose, be careful never to say anything against it, for fear of giving equal pain to others. Yet it would be a pity to leave the world ignorant of that experience which has moved my pen—the miracle of Sunday, October 6th, 1929.

You must know, then, that very many years ago, long before the Great War, and I think before Agadir of blessed memory, there came to my house an odd assortment of wine. It was not more than half a dozen, and each bottle of a separate kind. I can hardly remember how it came, but I seem to have some sort of idea that it was what is called "samples." Some wine merchant, generous and bent on trade, must have sent these bottles to me to choose amongst, that I might decide from which I should fill what Mr. Pooter in "The Diary of a Nobody" calls "my cellar." Anyhow, they lay there through the ages, and all things passed over them except a draught; for they were covered thicker and thicker with dust, as the slow years of peace and war and peace again—or truce—went creeping on seventeen years. 1912-1929! And the donor, I suppose, has gone to his felicity, and the letter which I presume he wrote has disappeared, and all record of that antiquity has perished.

It was by accident that I came upon that *cache* of a half-dozen. I was peering with a candle into the corner where they lay, looking for oil with which to make a salad, when I saw that venerable alignment with their earthy cloaks around them—the only things unchanged in a changing world. Through the thick coating which time had very gently laid upon them I could just read the lettering they bore. One was a wine of Anjou, which would to-day be water or vinegar. Another was from the Moselle. Upon a third was a simple label with the word "Larose." There was no year upon that label. No other wording at all: on the cork only brown wax.

I said to myself: "Claret is a doubtful thing. All the wines of the Garonne and of the Dordogne are as diverse as the souls and bodies of men. Some will live it out prodigiously for years, increasing in virtue with time—a process quite against the general order of things.

Some die young, and are soured by the wickedness of this world in their first bloom. Some with precocity attain ripeness early like the poets, and hang on like the poets doubtfully, preserving their main quality on into middle age, and then, like the poets, rapidly become intolerably dull, downright bad, and worthy of destruction: sometimes calling for vengeance. Others have so little substance in them, that they rot from the first. Some few, some very few, are worthy to be called contemporaries with man himself."

As I said this to myself, I remembered a wine of 1870, born in the same year as myself, a twin brother; a little older than my windmill, a little older than my boat; but we were all four, wine, man, windmill, boat, much of an age. This wine I had bought in Leadenhall Street, and it was fifty years old before I drank a drop of it; and it remained admirable to the end. So I communed with my own dear heart, and I said:

"Let us see what has happened to this Larose."

I took it out very gently, lest I should disturb its sleep and spoil its temper by a rough awakening. I stood it up in a far corner of a warm room, upon a little desk that is there, where it could have a background of sundry writers: a school textbook of the *Iliad; item*, another ditto of the *Odes* of Horace; an *Antigone* from the same days and dates; an *Asmodeus* of Le Sage in French which a friend had given me, and another in English; two Rabelais of the same sort; two Michelins of the same French sort, and a third yellow one for Spain; Yeats's *Wanderings of Oisin*, and a book called *The Outer Darkness*, which is all about the Queen of Hell, an old companion—and many others. There stood this row of books; there stood they and looked on the wine. And I sat down opposite and looked on it too, remembering many things. Then some friends came, and we had our meal, drinking that kind of wine called Lagune, with a good strong body and of sufficient development. But when the meal was over, I said to these friends of mine (they were five in number, all told, making six with myself, their host), "I have in the next room a bottle of which I know nothing, except that it is a claret and has slept without so much as turning for nearly twenty years. It may now be worthless, but I will open it for an experiment." Six is a prodigious number to share one bottle. It is like turning a squadron of horse on to one tin trough of water. But two of them I knew would take but a sip, so the main work would be attacked by only four. Yet four is a great number for one bottle of wine.

It was at the coronation of George IV, I think, or possibly of Queen Victoria, that the public were feasted at tables of four, with one bottle to a table, so that many sang to the tune of the National Anthem:

> Happy and glorious,
> One bottle among four of us,
> The devil send no more of us.

Moreover, I may tell you that I was not going to stint myself as host. I will never admit that the Host should go short of wine for the sake of his guests. It has always seemed to me that such sacrifice was too expensive and worth more than its God. For the God of Hospitality is hardly worth that abominable feeling of insufficiency in wine.

The cork, then, was drawn with very great care indeed, as one would deal with some issue concerning the life of a man. The rim, whence it had come out very sound and dark, was dusted with the utmost delicacy, and the Unknown was poured out as gently as the first words of lovers.

Immediately upon tasting it our humanity, there and then, blessed beyond the limits that are proper to a man in this life, knew that it had come upon something of Paradise.

Are you expecting me to describe that beatitude? Are you awaiting one of those paragraphs which sundry continentals of the nineteenth century excelled in—the attempt to put in words what is not proper to words but rather to the glory of the senses of man? Are you eager for just those terms in just that order which might call up some "simulacrum" of such real joy? You will be disappointed. I do not believe the thing can be done. I, at any rate, cannot do it. It transcends my power—of which I cannot boast in such affairs; and what is more, I verily believe and would swear that to describe that miraculous wine exceeds the powers of any mortal man that ever was born to breathe and move upon this unhappy earth.

⋆ XXIX ⋆

On Having One's Portrait Painted

I HAD intended, after writing this title (and one should never change a title), to write, as you may well imagine, upon the theme of Having My Portrait Painted. But whenever I use the words "Portrait" and "Painting" together, things crowd in upon me so fast that I do not know where to begin, and that I am tempted to run off down seventeen ways at once, like a dog trying to find a scent.

For one thing, it is always a miracle to me how any mortal can make a picture of another. It is a miracle, for that matter, how anyone can draw anything; how the order can be communicated from the eye through that mysterious little dæmon who lives, some say in the head, some on the top of the spine, down so clumsy a thing as a shoulder, and along so clumsy a thing as an arm, and so to a clumsy blob of a finger—which order can be so exactly obeyed that to within the hundredth of an inch the lines come true. In the case of trees, hills, boats, waves, the easier sorts of birds (notably the gull) and even some animals including the sheep, I am so familiar with the miracle myself that it has ceased to astonish me. I myself can communicate the order to reproduce the outline of a mountain, and it gets down on the paper so well that all its˙ friends will recognise it at once.

But when it comes to painting a human head with its expression, or modelling, or drawing the same, it astonishes me to the limits of astonishment how on earth the thing can be done. Yet the number of people who can do it, more or less, is infinite; and the number of people who can do it really well is so enormously larger than the number of people who want to pay for it, that many excellent portrait- and bust-makers of both sexes are at this very moment starving to death.

Then there is another matter. Is it wise to have one's portrait painted at all? It was but this morning I, being in a great hurry not to be late for an appointment, sauntered through a narrow passage and lingered over a number of old pictures in a shop window: pictures of notable men and women of the nineteenth century, the early part of the middle thereof; and I said to myself, "Lord! If they could see themselves now!"

For indeed, the greater part of these rich people (they were all rich except the writers among them) looked as perfect a set of guys as you could hope to meet in a month of travel. There are exceptions, I know. But I beg leave to believe that the exceptions were due to the talent of the artist and not to the character of the face he drew. The expression of a past age is commonly absurd because pride is a vice which warps the judgment. Now pride compels every man and woman sitting for a portrait in the year so-and-so (the year 1931, for instance) to put on such an air as they think will overawe posterity with their magnificence. Some will affect beauty, others strength, others breeding, others grandeur of soul, others (I am sorry to say) holiness; and how ludicrously they fail! I knew one man who had his portrait painted and drawn and a bust made of him and several caricatures and an etching, and as he sat for each of these he put on what he believed to be an air of terrifying ferocity which should make him go down to the future as a fellow not to be trifled with; one who knew what he wanted and got it; one before whom his fellows trembled. But the only result he got was to make himself appear repulsively ugly and a coward at heart.

So also the ladies, especially the great ladies. They simper in a thousand different ways, and I knew one who even attempted to express by a secret, ironical smile her capture and dismissal of men's hearts. But it had the effect of making her look that which no man can tolerate—I mean, a thoroughly empty-headed woman. Give me rather the Ugly Duchess.

Of which I hear, by the way, that some town council or politician or censorship or other tried to suppress the reproduction, lest it should corrupt youth.

There is one kind of portrait which seems to me exceptional as a real success in the way of bamboozling and impressing the time after the sitter's death, and that is the fine and careful pencil work of the 'fifties.

The men of that time, divines and Cabinet ministers and authors, used to have their pictures done in this way, and you may see them hanging on the walls of many a country house, where they remain not only an increasing delight, but an increasingly strong basis for legend. These pencil drawings of the mid-century (I would quote examples save that I might offend the living) nearly always make the fellow out to be that exact mixture of the sage, the hero, and the saint which every man thinks himself also to be. I have one in my mind's eye now, of a Secretary of State, who, not only by general repute and tradition within my own family (a sure guide), but even by his own horrible confessions in diaries and letters, still to be seen, though not printed, was one of the biggest scoundrels unhung. But his noble and lovely lineaments continue from the wall of a delightful old study in the Midlands to bless and uphold his great-great-nephews and nieces.

They are in no error. They are not deceived. In their intimate conversation they expose him and revile him, with a vigour and accuracy which give me infinite joy. There is always something new to be told about this abominable man. Only a few weeks ago I was gratified with another story of his appalling wickedness—how he had threatened with the revelation of a secret thing a colleague that he might bend him to his will. But he shines there, grey upon white, with an eye so beneficent, so tolerant and yet so just, with lips so firm yet modulated to the best accents of human speech, with a brow so majestic and hair of such ambrosial kind, that he might be a god baptized into the better Christian mood. If ever I sit for my portrait again I will try and get hold of someone who can do that sort of thing; but I doubt whether it will be possible. The breed is probably extinct. It was called into existence by the desire for record in the days before photography, or when photography was still thought to be what it still most certainly is, vulgar.

Which reminds me that the common tag about a photograph never revealing a personality is only half true. A snapshot will sometimes do it. But even the worst photograph, if it has not been faked, tells you more hidden things about the personality than the run of oils and drawings and marbles and bronzes. At any rate, it tells you more about the bad side. And that is the side one wants to hear about.

I conclude with a piece of advice to my generation, based upon experience. They may not know it (but I can tell them through ample experience) that verses are never written to a person. Of love verse this is especially true. It is written first in the void, and then, maybe, tacked on to a person, or maybe not. (So do not flatter yourselves, you Naiads, nor you, my fleeting visions of the summer dawns: it was not written to you at all: not a line of it.)

Now, might it not be so with portraiture? Suppose a man to be a good artist. A rich man commissions him to paint a portrait of that rich man's wife. You can see from here what she is really like. Let the artist avoid her presence; let him be off to a place called Las Planas, high in the wooded hills, and there, where the Muse lives and visits the unhappy race of men, let him paint loveliness. Then let him call it "Portrait of Lady Gowf," and if old Gowf won't pay for it he is a fool. Thus and thus only can the sum of beauty be maintained and the wicked custom of endowing posterity with hideous things be abolished.

★ XXX ★

Advice to a Young Man

MY DEAR young man. You need advice. I will give you some. If you are wise you will take it.

You were born in my own station of life, that is, in the over-cultivated and penniless middle-class. You have been trained to no profession. You have been to a public school. You have passed with or without distinction through one of those two old Universities the wide and profound learning of which is the envy of Europe. You find yourself with the modern world before you and you know not what to do. I will tell you.

Let us begin with the most important thing in life, which is money. If you have not yet appreciated the truth that money is everything, you soon will. You cannot to-day be so much as a free man without it; lacking money you can exercise no choice, you are a bound servant; or, if you do not accept that condition, you are a rebel and suffer the pains of the rebel. All that you may have imagined to be somehow superior to money—culture or taste, the tone of the friends to whom you are accustomed, necessary leisure, choice, every kind of travel and experience—has for a first necessity money. Far more important, money alone brings you the respect of your fellow beings. It has been well said that a man's standing with his fellows depends upon three factors, all of them turning upon money: (1) With how much money he is connected: (2) How long it has been possessed by the family: (3) How long it is likely to remain in their possession. Still more important, money is the basis of your own respect for yourself, without which man's life is steeped in irremediable misery. There is no such thing to-day as a life of proud poverty. You may enjoy it to the most for a few hours, or, if you are very lucky, a few days, between your beginning of the experiment and your condemnation by the lawyers to your first term of imprisonment. Do not attempt it.

From all this you may perhaps rashly conclude that money in the largest possible amount should be your object, and that I am about to make public the rules for its attainment (which you hope to be so simple that even you can grasp them). Here you err. I am about to do nothing of the sort. Though it is true that in proportion to the amount of money you have are you admired, respected and even loved by your fellow citizens, yet it is not true that in the same proportion do you acquire respect for yourself and that inner satisfaction, that moderate leisure, and, in general, that negative happiness which we all seek. For the attainment of these what is required is no very great sum, but a sufficiency for living one's life among one's fellows after the fashion in which one has been brought up and with a margin ample enough to educate a child or two and to leave each with a lucrative profession or an independence.

To say that, with a competence of this kind (say under post-war conditions £2,000 a year) you will satisfy ambition or even be looked up to by your fellows would be ridiculous, but with it you avoid embarrassment. It is embarrassment that kills a man, in mind and body and soul. It is embarrassment that breeds overwork, worry, dependence and the bitter self-reproach of dependence.

Here you will say, "Surely, since the larger the sum the greater the respect and glory, I should strain for the largest possible sum?" No: for in the attempt you risk far more than you gain. In every age the attainment of very great fortune has implied this condition. It has always been buying a pound for thirty shillings. To-day these vast amounts are to be attained only by various forms of theft and swindling of which the commonest is the using of special knowledge or judgment (real or imagined) for making others sell things to you far below their true value and yourself selling things to them far above the true value. Now it is a necessary part of this game that the winners (who make the laws and whom the system of justice and police is organised to serve) shall make it as difficult as possible for another to filch what they have obtained. Therefore, by a pretty paradox, precisely the same tricks which procure a man great fortune if they just come off, land him in gaol or in the gutter if they do not. I have lived long and watched many men, my contemporaries. Of those few who began life with the fixed determination to accumulate great sums, not one in ten has reached later middle age without grave misfortune. Of these only a minority have actually passed through prison, but the rest would violently admit that the game had proved disastrous for them. So leave it alone.

Well, then, about that competence. Marry a woman who is a widow, childless and possessed of sufficient means. Let her be of your own rank—perhaps a trifle above it, but not greatly so; even (if she have the advantage of very large means) slightly below it—but at least with nothing remarkable in the way of accent or manner. Choose her for judgment and good temper: the two requisites (and the only two) necessary to prolonged agreement. The poet Hesiod laid it down that the man should be about ten years older than the woman. But I tell you that the woman should be about ten years older than the man. Why a widow? Because she will understand men, she will not be too impatient of your selfishness and folly, and you will be compelled to respect her, which is necessary in the relations of men to women and even in some degree in those of women to men. Be sure that she will soon bring you to a state in which she will be able to pay even to you some degree of respect.

Associate with the rich; study them carefully; flatter them after the fashion which they individually enjoy and collectively demand. All the rich demand flattery, but one likes a spice of opposition, another bold adulation, a third some considerable intervals of neglect, or (let us say) of repose from your society. But while you associate with the rich, never make their society necessary to you, and never acquire from them habits which would strain your resources. Thus it is as well not to shoot, save very rarely; but you may ride occasionally (if you can acquire the art) and certainly you may practise billiards, lawn tennis and all those other great activities which mark the governing classes of the State. Bridge, of course, is indispensable.

Neither give nor lend money with that loose emotion called "charity." It is a vice which grows on men and leads to infinite complications. Forbear to *give* one penny to individuals. *Lend* a little discreetly here and there, not with the object of relieving the borrower, but with some definite object of your own, such as a reputation with him or his attachment; or even (if you desire it) his absence. Write a little verse. Do not try to make it good, for you will fail; but see that it be not below a certain standard. For thoroughly bad verse renders men ridiculous, and to be ridiculous is to be damned. In this connection let me warn you against the epigram, the witty tale, and above all, a general jocularity. Men are only too willing to enjoy the amusement afforded by the buffoon, but they will treat him with increased contempt the more he serves them. In the matter of wine, confine yourself to champagne. If it makes you ill, drink little of it; but drink *some*, you must. The habit common to the rich of pumping it up and down to get the bubbles out you will find a great help and comfort through your brief life and especially with the advance of years. As for red wine it is silly to pretend any knowledge of it. Your contemporaries have long lost the faculty of taste in wine. It is merely literature, and if you really know good wine when you come across it you are an eccentric, and you might as well be a foreigner at once.

Accept insult. The phantom "honour" is a source

of untold misfortune to those who cling to it. But to do you justice I do not think you will be under any temptation in this regard. Insult in the modern world is rare, and when you have grown accustomed to occasional doses of it, you will hardly notice the taste. Run no man down, not even the poor, not even the dead; and here I would add a very hard commandment, but one the observance of which is essential. Do not even discuss other people behind their backs, save in the way of praise. This rule is particularly to be observed in the case of villains, and more particularly of those villains who steal public money, or in general abuse their position as public servants. Praise men according to their power; but praise all—remembering, however, not to wander into enthusiasm. And while you are praising, remember to praise a man for those talents in which you have noticed that he desires to shine but cannot. In this way you will make all men your friends at no expense save of integrity.

The time will come, my dear young friend, when, after the process of a life thus well spent, you will begin to feel the approach of a shadow, which is that of Death. Do not let it occupy your mind. Study carefully the health of your body, taking care to learn from your wealthier friends the names of specialists skilful in propping up and patching the teeth, the nose, the throat, the stomach, and other organs. Yet (and this is no light task) manage all the while to keep your mental visage turned away from the grave and those insoluble problems which it is a folly to attempt. By this I do not mean that you should ridicule the illusions of others, or such old-fashioned doctrines as may still survive among them, as, of a Heaven, a Hell, a God and even a Saviour. There is nothing upon which fools are more sensitive. But for yourself be rid of such whimsies altogether.

Do not tell me that it is impossible to avoid some consideration of your end. On the contrary, you may see the forgetfulness of it most successfully accomplished upon every side. An excellent tip, when you are finding the struggle too hard, is to take up some hobby, not too expensive, such as, to collect editions of one lesser author of the past (such as Horace), or Rumanian pottery. Stamps are out of date.

I have nothing to add save my sincere good wishes for your unfaltering conduct in such a life as I have prescribed for you, and my mournful assurance that though, towards its close, you will feel yourself not a little disappointed, you will at least have escaped the agonies, as also, of course, the triumphs and the visions and all the rest of them.

Farewell, and do not trouble me again.

★ XXXI ★

On Writing as a Trade

Mr. Arnold Bennett did me the honour to write, some months ago, an important article in the *Evening Standard*, taking for his text a phrase of mine in the *Cruise of the Nona* to the effect that a man was not meant to live by his pen. He maintains the opposite with great strength, and was generous enough to quote part of my own work in evidence.

He was in exceedingly good company, and the shade of Dr. Johnson applauded him.

Now, I would not maintain the opposite as a complete thesis, nor expand that chance original sentence of mine into a full affirmation that the burden of writing for what is foolishly called "one's bread" (but is more exactly the whole bundle of necessaries and luxuries and follies which make up a modern life) is merely evil. But I confess that though I have turned the matter over continually in my mind since that article of Mr. Bennett's appeared, I continue to incline to the belief that the bulk of men and women who have to write for an income suffer from that constraint, and that literature as a whole suffers still more when its professors are thus all, or nearly all, professional.

The arguments on the other side are very strong. The strongest, perhaps, is that which M. Bennett advanced, with a quick grasp of the main point, that the creative temperament is lazy—as a rule. Let us suppose that even out of a thousand writers but one has creative power— that is, can bring forth something in prose or verse which is a worthy possession for his fellows, and a permanent one. That one creative exceptional man or woman will, as a rule, not undertake the effort of creation without direct economic necessity as an incentive. At any rate, he will not as a rule break himself in to the business— though after he is broken in he will, as we know, continue for other and better motives, less servile and worthier of his talent. It follows that, if people did not write for gain, the few writings that are worth having would for the most part never have appeared. That is true. And it is as true of the old days of patronage as it is true of the modern days of competition. If it be advanced that, with writing become a trade for thousands, the great mass of what is written is worthless, the answer immediately arises that the worthless stuff can be neglected, and only the worthy stuff will count.

But against considerations as clear and as convincing as these, there are two points in the psychology of the writer which rather support my attitude. In the first place, though the creative temperament is usually lazy, it is also on occasion a compelling force of itself; and that especially in youth, when most of the best stuff is written. It is certainly so with verse, and good verse I take to be the highest expression of the craft. A man does not write good verse for money. It can't be done. Say to a man whom Olympus has dowered with its pure gold (there is not one good poet out of a million men, and there is no good poet who is always good): "Write me something as good as your Threnody on the late Mr. Posselthwaite, M.P., and I will give you a thousand pounds." He will reply, if he is honest, "You might offer me ten thousand—it would make no difference."

With prose it is otherwise—even with good prose, though hardly with that very high form called rhetoric. Good rhetoric is rare and capricious of inspiration. If you try to compel it you fall into the depths; for jaded rhetoric is intolerable. But straightforward prose, well put together, doing its plain work, a work essential to the State, can be written even at its best under the mere incentive of gain. I am not so sure that it can be written under the incentive of *competitive* gain; and here there enters a consideration which I feel to be of great weight. It is this: there is not in the writing of prose any natural check. That is why such masses of it are turned out at so grievously insufficient a price. The price may often be more than the stuff is worth. It usually is. But it is woefully too small for security and peace of mind. Much the most of the great army that are to-day living or trying to live by their pen live under an anxiety and strain, an insecurity and a loss of self-respect, worse than in any other calling I can review. It was written, I think by More, that there ought not to be more clerks in the commonwealth than there is provision for by endowment. The judgment has always seemed to me wise. Balzac said a very true thing when he maintained that the writing man gives more of himself than any other kind of worker. He is the pious pelican; he feeds the brutish populace upon his own flesh. I doubt whether there is any interval more dispiriting than that between the moment when a man sets out in his fatigue to attempt *some* writing, utterly indisposed to it and only, because it is his miserable task (hardly even a duty, certainly not a natural activity, but a bitter, slavish compulsion) and that when, perhaps an hour later, he has screwed himself up to the pitch. No wonder they drink!

The other point is that competitive payment tends to be by length; or perhaps I should say, competitive commercialised payment tends to be by length—and that is frankly ridiculous. There is no sort of connection between volume and excellence in this particular activity. There is even less connection between volume and excellence than there is in the other arts, and we all know how little there is in painting, for instance. Who would judge the value of a picture by its acreage? Yet the commercial support of the writing man fatally tends to be thus measured. The bookseller, the publisher, the editor, even the more intelligent of the public will say of a short thing—"It seems a lot to have to pay for such a little" . . . as might be the Gospel of St. John, or the *Donec Gratus Eram Tibi* of Horace, which for my part I cannot read, even the hundredth time, without an approach to tears. What would Horace have made of that poem, by the way, if Mæcenas had taken him aside and said, "You know, when you asked for five pounds, I expected something longer than that! You must add to it!"

And in this connection there occurs to me yet another evil, which is the standardisation of length.

That does not matter in things of set form, such as an

179

essay, or a sonnet, a ballade, or a good piece of leader-writing; but I think it does matter in books. I have myself insisted upon writing sundry books for my own pleasure, which were below the regulation size. I don't deny that I have been sympathetically treated by the publishers, and even the purchasers, of such books. But there was always thought to be something odd about them, like a dwarf on parade. Strangely enough, by the way, that doesn't seem to apply to excessive length, but only to concision; so that we should have difficulty to-day in pushing *Daphnis and Chloe*, but every chance of unloading *Clarissa*.

Well, let me conclude with the mournful satisfaction that it has to be, and that I for my part can't complain. But I do insist that the trade is a hard one. When Mr. Bennett told us, very truly, that indolence was the besetting sin of the artist, I think he knew, as I do, why it is so. It is because of that strain in action which most men who can create so acutely feel. Pay for pay, I would much rather dig, groom horses, haul at ropes, or in any other fashion fatigue the body.

Yet there is one great compensation. I should be ungrateful not to set it down at the end of this random moan. We writing hacks have freedom. Pray allow me to be personal again; it is not fashionable, but I find it much the easiest way of saying a thing. A couple of years ago I wanted to write about James II. I went off to the edge of the Sahara Desert and wrote the book in not many consecutive days in a jolly little bungalow hotel that I know of on the banks of a stream coming down from Aurès. Now, I could not have edited a paper, built a house, audited an account, or acted the part of

Hamlet (before paying audiences) in that remote residence by the palm grove.

So God be praised! But in that book there were innumerable slips of the pen and half a dozen good, honest howlers, the fruits of hermitage and liberty.

★ XXXII ★

The Death of the Ship

THE other day there was a ship that died. It was my own ship, and in a way I would it had not died. But die it had to, for it was mortal, having been made in this world: to be accurate, at Bembridge, in the Isle of Wight, nearly sixty years ago. Moreover, since boats also must die, it is right that they should die their own death in their own element; not violently, but after due preparation; for, in spite of modern cowardice, it is better to be prepared for death than unprepared.

They may tell me that a ship has no being at all; that a boat is not a person, but is only a congeries of planks and timbers and spars and things of that sort. But that is to open up the whole debate, undecided, branched out, inexhaustible, between realism and nominalism—on which I wish you joy.

She was my own boat, and I knew her very well, and I loved her with all my heart. I will offer you speculation on whether, now she has dissolved her being in this world of hers—which was sand and mud, salt water, wind and day and night and red and green lights, and harbours far away—she shall not be a complete boat again with all her youth upon her, in the paradise of boats. You may debate that at your leisure.

She had been patched up for years past. So are men in their old age and their decay. As the years proceeded she had been more and more patched up. So are men more and more patched up as the years proceed. Yet all those who loved her tried to keep her going to the very last. So it is with men.

But my boat was happier than men in this, that no one desired her death. She had nothing to leave, except an excellent strong memory of days calm, days windy, days peerless, days terrific, days humorous, days empty in long flats without a breath of wind, days beckoning, principally in the early mornings, leading on her admirable shape, empress of harbours and of the narrow seas. Also, she had no enemies, and no one feared her. There was no one to say, as there is of men, "I shall be glad when they are out of the way." There was no one to wish her that very evil wish which some men do other men—themselves evil: "I am glad to think that he is dead."

No. My boat went most honourably and straightly to her death. She had nothing to repent, nothing to regret, nothing to fear, nothing to be the cause of shame. It is so with things inanimate, and, indeed, with animals. It is so with everything upon this earth, except man.

My boat was the best sea-boat that ever sailed upon the sea. The reason of this was that her lines were of the right sort, belonging, as they did, to the day when England was England; and my boat was so English that if you had seen her in any foreign port you would have known at once that you had seen an English thing. But, indeed, nowadays, what with their boats made like spoons and their boats made like table knives, and their boats made like tops, and their boats made like scoopers, and their boats made like half-boats, cut away in the middle, no one can tell whether a boat is Choctaw, Esquimaux, or Papuan. For boats have nowadays fallen into chaos, like everything else.

But this boat was plumb English, cod-fish nose and mackerel stern. She was, between perpendiculars, 29½ foot. She was, over all, 36 foot. She was of cutter rig, she was 9 tons—according to the only measurement worth having, and fancy measurements may go to the devil. Four men were happy on board her, five men she could carry, six men quarrelled. She did not sail very close to the wind, for she was of sound tradition and habit, the ninth of her family, and perhaps the last. To put her too close was to try her, and she did not like it. But she would carry on admirably four points off, and that is all you need in any boat, I think. She drew from just over to just under 6 foot, according to the amount of human evil there was aboard her and of provision therefor. And she never, never failed.

She never failed to rise to a sea, she never failed to take the stiffest or most sudden gust. She had no moods or tantrums. She was a solid, planted thing. There will be no more like her. The model is broken. There was a day when I should have cared very much. Now I am glad enough that she is gone down the dark way from which, they say, there is no return. For I should never have sailed her again.

He who had designed the lines of her approached the power of a creator, so perfect were they and so smooth and so exactly suited to the use of the sea. For modern men would have made her, no doubt, with a view to speed or with a view to holding this or that, or having this or that luxury aboard; to finding a place aft for the abomination of an engine. But those who made her knew nothing of all these things. They made her to be married to the sea.

As to speed, I suppose she never in her life made nine full knots in one hour. (As for those who say you cannot sail so many "knots" in an hour, and that the expression is inaccurate, because a knot is not the same thing as a sea mile—my feeling about them is so strong that I dare not express it in words; so I leave it at that.) I say I doubt if she ever made nine knots in the hour, even on that famous day when she ran violently over-canvassed because she had jammed a block, roaring from the flats east of Griz Nez to the flats of Romney in just over three hours, not knowing whither she went, nor I either until the land was suddenly upon us—as suddenly as the land had left us when we first rushed out into that thick weather—and that, God help me! was more than a quarter of a century ago.

In a good breeze, and behaving with comfort and tradition, she might make seven knots: or, again, one and a half. I have known her go out of Salcombe of a Saturday on the first of the ebb at noon, and make Torquay on the Monday morning with an oiled calm in between. On the other hand, she once ran me from that same Torquay to the Solent in less time than it takes a man to betray his loyalties or to deny his God: or, at least, in less time than it takes him to change his habits in the way of treason.

She once took me round from Dorsetshire to Cornwall one summer night and with a wind off the land which was much too strong in passing Bolt Head; and she has taken me here and she has taken me there; and now we are to part—if not for ever, at any rate for a good many weeks or months or years. Which things, I suppose, are inconsiderable to Eternity. No matter. We part.

The patching up had got more and more difficult. It had had to be renewed more and more often. The expense was nothing. We will always pay for doctors when it is a matter of those we love. But off the Norman coast the other day she gave me that look which they give us before they leave us, and she started a plank. It was high time. Had she not been near the piers it might have gone hard with those on board. But she got through, though the Channel was pouring in, and she reached the basin within, her cock-pit half full, and then lay up upon the mud. And there she did what corresponds in man to dying. She ceased to be a boat for the purposes of a boat any longer. She was no-longer-patch-up-able. She had fulfilled her task. It was all over. She had taken to her repose.

Very soon she with hammer and wedge was dissolved into her original elements—all that was mortal of her—and the rest is on the seas of paradise.

I wish I were there—already: now: at once: with her.

XXXIII

Buckingham

THERE is a man who remains insufficiently explained to his compatriots. He might have been a national hero. He has just failed from being made a stage villain and, in between, he remains too vague. He does not fill the stage as he should. He is not, even for those who blame him, a figure as solid or as large as he should be. For the very few who praise him he is even more tenuous. This man is George Villiers, Duke of Buckingham.

It is true that in this misfortune which his name has suffered of receiving less than its due attention, the incongruities of his life, not wholly explicable, play some part; for men like to have their villains or their heroes simple and of a piece—it saves them the trouble of appreciation, of exactitude, and of admitted mystery (for mystery is something which it takes much humility and therefore strength of mind to accept).

But then (though he had more incongruity attaching to him than have most men) no historical character, no humble individual, is without many such contradictions; and if it had been fated that Buckingham should be one of the great national figures set up for exaggerated adoration, or exaggerated anathema, the incongruities would have been eliminated easily enough by our popular historians, novelists, examiners, and the rest of the tribe, glaring though these incongruities were.

He was certainly not vicious: I think one can accept that. But as certainly he lent himself to the disgusting fondles of Darnley's neurotic and slouching son. Being then of such antecedents at court, one would have thought that the next reign would have taken its revenge—especially as Charles was the most virtuous of English Kings. Yet Charles felt for him that strong, manly and fixed affection which did both men honour. It was one of the very rare cases of a father's favourite succeeding to the position of favourite with his son. He was related to Catholicism and indeterminate in religion at a moment when a real triangular duel was afoot between the Roman communion, the Establishment, and Calvinism. This was not in him exceptional at such a time, but there is something incongruous in his acceptation of full public responsibility unaccompanied by an equally full declaration of his attitude. Probably he would have ended upon the Roman side of the hedge had things gone that way: certainly not on the Calvinist, had he survived to see things go, as they did go, *that* way. It is incongruous in our eyes (though less so in the eyes of his time) that a great soldier should be half dandy and half magnificent. But perhaps the most incongruous accident was the very passionate and real love affair with Anne of Austria.

There was no national policy about that amour. There was no simple taking advantage of a neglected woman. It was a violent and compelling flame. You cannot read the evidence of contemporaries without seeing that. Yet how could it be excited in such a man by such a woman?

I repeat, all those incongruities would have been smoothed over by official history had things gone otherwise with him than they did. And how nearly did they go well! What determined his fate was the expedition in relief of the Huguenots. Because he failed in that, he has turned into the wandering ghost he is; and that upstanding, manly, English, martial figure floats pale and ill-defined.

The decision to land upon the Isle de Rhé was wise, quite certainly; as was also wise in policy the diversion in favour of the Huguenots. For the diversion in favour of the Huguenots was a sop to the hugely menacing growth of power in the squires and the great mercantile interests. Those classes had gone far already in undermining the Crown. Had Buckingham's expedition succeeded, the success would have compelled the House of Commons (the committee and impersonation of those classes), to grant aid to that old, regular and feudal subsidy which had become hopelessly insufficient for the conduct of the State. A great Navy would have been built for the English Crown, and a tax for it readily admitted. Had Buckingham come back triumphant from that expedition, monarchy might have survived, and government by the rich, and all the Whig theory, might never have matured.

It is one of the great "ifs" of history. But Buckingham's failure was not the failure of bad generalship. It came from just that lack of fortune which even to the best of generals means the difference between defeat and victory. He was perfectly right in seizing the Isle de Rhé. Not only was the Isle de Rhé the key to La Rochelle (with the English established in Rhé, and able to be reinforced and to attack, the town would never have fallen), but, possessed by a maritime power, it could have been held indefinitely. It would have been a permanent base off the coast of a rival. It was no foolhardy attempt. With the exception of a company or two behind the insufficient works of one fort, all the island had to offer was the tiny walled town of St. Martin—ill-garrisoned, with defences in decay, insufficiently provisioned: commanded, it is true, by a man of exceptional capacity and vigour—for Toiras was all that—but with heavy odds against its standing out. The stroke had the full element of surprise, which is the first essential of success in war. To meet it no French maritime force as yet existed. It failed in that "last quarter of an hour" which the epigram of Foch has rendered famous in modern ears. The accident of foul weather following on a storm which had damaged the boom and, much more, the accident of a dense fog immediately coinciding with a high spring tide, permitted those few Basque pinnaces to throw in at the very last moment just the bare extra munitionment which enabled the besieged garrison to hold out till the forces of the King of France should be organised.

When Buckingham came home he was a defeated man. He had left behind him in dead, wounded and captured, the better part of the thousands of Englishmen and the few hundreds of French Protestants who had made the effort. But, though defeated, his military reputation should in justice have remained untarnished. The Gods had defeated him.

Such justice is rarely done to any defeated commander. Yet he still maintained his energy, his determination and his plan. When he was murdered, he was upon the eve of renewing action and negotiation, and we may be sure, from his character and his intelligence, that he would have again collected with judgment all the conditions of success. But, with Buckingham dead, the entire plan collapsed. That hatred which his name had inspired seemed justified in the event; and perhaps Charles himself, who had, like all the Stuarts, from the days of the mediæval curse upon them (in their own country), odd fits of prescience, knew when the news came to him, hunting in the big wood behind Portsdown, that his own evil star had arisen. For it is from the murder of Buckingham that all the future flows. That half-crazy, disappointed man who stabbed the Duke started by that one gesture a mighty flood of consequence which fills the history of England.

Buckingham had been hated from that convergence of causes which made such men standing at the side of monarchy hated in the mighty debate between monarchy and great subject-interests which is the duel of the seventeenth century throughout Europe. There was still such sacredness about Kingship that bad advisers must be blamed rather than the King himself; while, for the mass of men, it is necessary (in order that they may be saved the trouble of thinking) to have one name upon which to concentrate as the simple cause of all which incommodes them. So it is, for a certain sort of fanatic, the Jew or the Jesuit or the Freemason, or Boney, or the

Jacobin, or the Pope of Rome, or 666, or some harmless strike-leader, or what not. On Buckingham concentrated these obvious causes of hate. But had he come back triumphant, that hate would have stood no chance with the general spirit of England. He would have come back a conqueror in a popular cause, a conqueror upon the English element of the sea, and a conqueror national in his character, virtues and foibles. It is not the least remarkable thing about his memory, nor the least proof of his capacity, that the common legend against him never took sufficient root to make him lurid. But perhaps his spirit, if it still remembers these things of long ago, or cares for the earth of the Parks of Amiens and of St. James's, would prefer to be enshrined in general execration, than to have fallen to the void wherein his legend now lies.

XXXIV

On Books as Wares

MEN complain, justly enough, that the production of books to-day is becoming *wholly* commercialised. At least, those men complain of the thing who have a right instinct in the matter and know how dangerous it is to the State that Letters should decline. That the making and selling of books must be on commercial lines is obvious. But the evil complained of is the decreasing admission of any other than the commercial factor, and the consequent peril to English Literature.

There is no doubt that the evil is happening, and there is little doubt that the evil will increase. Now, what you have to do with any evil is not simply to complain of it; but first to discover its cause, next to see how far, and in what way, it can be remedied.

By the commercialisation of books we mean essentially (though the phrase is not one appealing to the popular ear) the turning of books from a luxury into a necessary. I am not here using the terms "luxury" and "necessary" in the moral sense, but in the sense in which they were used by the old economists, who distinguished between that which was of general usage, calling it a necessity, and that which was of particular usage, calling it a luxury. In this sense boots are a necessity, though one can very well do without them, and it is healthy enough going barefoot; while good curtains to a sleeping-room are a luxury, although, to not a few men, their absence is intolerable. In the same way one might call the modern evening paper a necessary (which in the moral sense it certainly is not), and one might call a memorandum leading to the slavation of the State a "luxury." Of the first you must have many hundreds of thousands printed or you cannot produce it at all; of the second, half a dozen are enough, and they may be written by hand.

Well, then, in this sense, books have changed within our own time from being a luxury to being in the main a necessary.

The cause of this is generally made out to be universal compulsory instruction in the art of reading. That seems to me a misapprehension. In my boyhood I was brought up among plenty of people of the poorer sort, whose childhood dated from before the Act of 1870. Some were illiterate; but the number who could read was not very much less than it is to-day. I do not know how statistics would go, and even if there are any such printed I should not trust them, for I trust real experience far more. But, anyhow, the older England was not illiterate. Of the dependents about our household and those of my relatives all read the Bible, many the *Pilgrim's Progress*. The difference between that old England and the newer England is that people have by now fallen into a habit of *perpetual* reading, which in the better days the great mass of English men and women had not acquired. There is something comparable here to the habit of travel. Railways and steamboats were available for everyone forty years ago. Travel (especially by sea) was cheaper than it is now, in proportion to general incomes; but the habit of travel has got somehow into people's blood and changed the whole affair. So it has been with reading.

The economic consequences inevitable after such a change are fairly clear. The first is, that unless a book is selling briskly, it is not in general worth keeping alive. Storage space is expensive. Books are bulky things and heavy also. Where it paid a publisher to keep a book in stock and sell x copies a year, it now only pays him to keep a book in stock if he can still sell ten times x copies a year. He cannot afford to lose money on his business, and therefore only the period of lively sale can keep a book in existence. I speak only of the run of books; of course, for textbooks and one or two other special sorts, the rule does not apply.

There is another consequence. Not only does it not pay to keep the book alive, but it does not pay to issue the book at all unless it is to have a certain sale. The costs of travelling it and advertising it, and the rest, have gone up so largely with the increased figures that the minimum the publisher must sell in order to make a profit on an edition gets continually larger.

Meanwhile, the notices of books have become commercialised also. Roughly speaking, a book will not be reviewed unless it has been advertised in the paper which reviews it. There are exceptions, but that is the general commercial rule.

Lastly, a book to be published at all must be *expected* to appeal and, to be kept alive, must *actually* have appealed, to a very large public. It is silly to laugh at the large public; you and I are all part of it, and to pretend that it has a baser taste than you and I have is vanity. But what is true is that when it comes to very large numbers, people do not want profound matter. That is just as true of you and me as of the rest of the herd to which we belong. We use most reading for recreation, and we read what we are content to forget a few hours after reading it. We read graver matter, no doubt, but not on the same scale in mere numbers.

Put all that together and the conclusion you arrive at is that, under the conditions of to-day, in England at least, the issuing and maintenance of serious and permanent literature is heavily handicapped. The delay which may be necessary before recognition can be attained is lacking. The material has a better chance if it is ephemeral, or, at any rate, easy to read rapidly. The most serious consequence of all is, I think, this: many of the books which have been of the greatest moment have, in the past, pierced through by the zeal of a comparatively narrow circle. Many books of great moment have, indeed, had immediate fame and sale, but many also have not. Under modern conditions those which, in the past, established themselves slowly can now never establish themselves at all. Again, the number of those who judged was much smaller than it is to-day; and their judgment was better, because they had behind them a conscious tradition and the advantage of leisure. Again, the great modern State militates against accuracy and profundity of judgment. To all this must be added one further evil, and it is a very grave one. Men are content to judge the value of literary effort by the number of its readers and the money which its author earns.

Everyone will indignantly deny that this is his standard; but if you will narrowly watch the actions of men—which are the proof of their less conscious feelings—you will find that this is so. Great sales, and especially great *sudden* sales, are becoming a test of excellence. Large fortunes made out of modern fiction or play-writing are taking the place of that fame which once attached to the highest verse, the neatest wit, the finest rhetoric. It is also true that a certain proportion—a very small proportion, I admit—of first-rate matter goes by unnoticed and is lost. I take it that this is of grave disadvantage to the State; for the whole amount of first-rate matter in verse or prose is exceedingly small.

As for the remedies, it is clear that here, as in all other departments, you cannot create an economic remedy against an economic tendency. Your remedy must be uneconomic in some form. To correct an evil due to free economic action, you need something which counteracts economic action: as, for instance, when you keep a sick man alive. Your remedy, in plain English, must be to publish and criticise at a loss.

Now, if we are to check that decline of Letters which comes of economic tendency, we need a method which returns to books as a luxury. We need criticism that shall be endowed, and we need some department in the production of books which shall be endowed also; but we need the endowment of criticism more than we need the endowment of production. It is conceivable that a good circulating library, limited in the number of its subscribers, restricted by its constitution to a certain maximum of annual purchase, would (in the right hands) begin to help matters. But I can see that, when it comes to remedying any one of the modern evils attaching to haste and turmoil, constructive suggestion is very difficult, and perhaps nowhere more difficult than here.

My innermost thought in the matter is that the strongest force we can set to work towards a renaissance of taste is snobbishness. Once make people believe that a particular set or club or library has the goods, and that it is of high tone to deal with it, and you have some chance of restoring an aristocracy in Letters. Should such return, it would be full of nonsense, like all aristocracy, but it might achieve some few of an aristocracy's very necessary functions: one of which is continuity, and another selection.

★ XXXV ★

The Old Horse-bus

THE other day I happened to be passing in a car through a village somewhat remote in my own county. There is a railway station there; and as I started early from home, before I could buy a morning paper, I turned off to the station to get one. And there it was I saw a sight which made the world stand still and put an end to the torrent of the years. It was the old horse-bus of the place, which I had known in early youth, and which, before my astonished eyes, still lived. *Fies Nobilium tu quoque Horsebussorum*; for I will hymn you, Horse-bus of my heart.

Patience was in the bent heads of the horses, and humility and an honest human—I mean caballian or equine—appetite expecting the stable. For as those beasts waited the arrival of trains with one passenger, they munched at nothing upon their bits, and in their hearts remembered oats and hay.

All the blessing of the old world was upon that horse-bus, and I could look upon it without a renewal of my own youth, but a certitude that nothing is lost for ever.

There was hierarchy upon it (which the fever of the

199

modern world has for a moment destroyed). For there is the owner of it, Mr. Wugg, there is the driver of it, Mr. Staples, there is the ostler, Jonas, and Jonas has a slave of his own, and the slave has a boy who does the work. At least, so it was when I last saw that horse-bus at this same station all those years ago, when petrol was still an exceptional liquid and before the last excesses of machinery had begun to destroy us.

In that submission to hierarchy, in that contentedness with oats and hay, in that dignity of slow progress, was all the ancient world; and I said to those horses, "You are blessed, and you have your reward. Is it not so, Horses of the Horse-bus which used to run and (unless all this be a vision) still runs from Great Diggleton to Lower Speeding? You could bear witness, O Horses, if you were allowed. But luckily for you, you are not allowed. You are not pestered with the power of speech, and you are magnificently free from the temptations of the spirit. But if you could speak, you could tell us that you enjoy that ancient peace which goes with hierarchy, humility, a stable, leisure, contemplation—all those things."

I was tempted to wait until the train should come in, so as to see those sights and to hear those words which would have called up my childhood within me from the dead.

I was tempted to remain and see the one passenger get out—Mrs. Mowles, it used to be, now it would be some other, but of the same excellent sort, I am sure, which is as broad as it is long. That passenger would climb into the sacred vehicle, the car of undying things, and find there Mr. Joyce, the grocer, and even perhaps

Captain Ling taking the opportunity of a lift for half a mile.

How excellent would be the conversation! The grocer would complain of the weather. The Captain would condemn it. Mrs. Mowles would say, that one day with another, there was as much rain one year as another, and that it was all under Providence, wherein Mrs. Mowles would have said more than many books can say. Then they would have spoken of public affairs, of which they would have only known what their papers told them, and on which they would have commented with that simple patriotism which is almost a virtue, and which fills the mind with content.

But I did not wait for the train to come in, nor play the somewhat expensive time-wasting game of renewing an experience so many years dead, and solemnly driving back in the horse-bus, with the car, I suppose, following after like a hearse. It would have been ridiculous, it would have been affected. Nor, for that matter, can one ever revive good things defunct. I could not hope that by so acting I should recover the years that never will return.

Unless ghosts had come to fill shadowy places within the little ancient carriage—and who would invoke the presence of the dead?—those about me in it would have been strangers, and I should not really have recovered the famous horse-bus of old. I should not have forgotten, as it clattered along, that all about it was the roaring and the futility of the machines, and the murderous haste and the vibration, and the metallic clamour. I should not have escaped the evil of our degraded day.

Peace will return at long last, but after some fashion

we know not of. After great disasters, I fear perhaps after heavy conflict between rich and poor, or between alien and native; or perhaps after plague and famine and the destruction of letters and of art, and a descent into barbaric things.

Perhaps after such a bath and purgation Christendom will arise again in the quiet and the dignity that were once its glory.

But I can't get all that back simply by getting into the old horse-bus to Great Diggleton. No; I must abandon the false lure and resist the temptation, and let the horse-bus go, like some much-beloved name heard on the lips of others after thirty years.

What nobility there was in those days! How slowly came the evening, down upon the lanes and fields of my county—at a true hour fixed by the sun and the process of creation, not by the mechanical jugglery of man! With what beneficence as of a sacred word putting an end to stress and ill-ease, the mists and half-darknesses came on together over the vale between the great hills! There was no sound except the bells in the folds, or very far away the hoofs of a horse; and man, and the housing of man, his ways, the steeples of his worship, the smoke going up in the autumn air from his hearths—a smoke of fragrant oaken fires—all these were at one with what nature did around us, and joined together, whether they would or no, in a common act of peace and of solemn adoration until the night concluded all.

To-day these benedictions are destroyed, and peace has fled away in terror to better places. The roads are roaring avenues of death, the little towns are filled with a din as of some hellish factory. The new buildings are viler with false taste or vilest with a dead imitation of forgotten goodness. In the place of the candle-light behind the curtains in low rooms shining through small square panes you have the glare, the blue metallic torturing glare, of the new light which kills the darkness instead of softening and redeeming it. Of the old good nothing remains . . . except the horse-bus.

. . . Except the horse-bus of Great Diggleton. And in that symbol I repose. By it I see that something of antique virtue survives mysteriously above the flood, and I could almost believe that a Good Genius will preserve it immortal in its own place, until the better things return.

XXXVI

The Conversation of the Condemned

MARCUS: Gentlemen, it is evening. I shall ask for the lamps to be lighted. (*He claps his hands for a slave, and having done so, rearranges his raiment fastidiously. The slave enters and lights the lamps upon the walls.*) I have asked you to my house because I thought it more convenient.

GRATION: They say that there are doors to Hades in every house, and passages down from every field. But, as you say, Marcus, it is pleasanter to go in company.

MARCUS: I did not say that. For my part, I should have found it pleasanter to go alone. But I desired to see my friends. Do you not also desire me, on such a night, to be your host?

QUINTUS: Come, now, Marcus, this is no time for temper. We are all beholden to you. First, that you have given us the opportunity to be with you at the end, in this noble house, but next that you have given us the opportunity to be all together.

PERTINAX: At any rate it has saved the Master a great deal of trouble. He would have had to send a centurion to each house, and as I have not even got a house, but only a lodging, in a second-rate street, it has also saved the centurion a little embarrassment. For the lower middle class do not like to be seen on vulgar errands, especially in uniform.

QUINTUS: For my part, I should have hated to hear them keeping step and grounding arms in my little hall. Besides which, it would have disturbed my mother. She always says that in her time people never called at a gentleman's house without sending warning. But she also adds that one never knows what we are coming to.

MARCUS: Yes, Quintus, times have changed. But even in my grandfather's day a company of soldiers would appear now and then with certain orders to a gentleman: and even in those days the orders had to be obeyed.

GRATION: When the order comes, we shall obey it sure enough.

PERTINAX: All you fine fellows know more about these things than I do. Can you not give me a hint as to how it will be worded? Will they march us out and cut off our heads before daylight, beyond the walls? Or will they bring round a cup, out of which we all shall drink? Or what?

MARCUS: We are still gentlemen, I hope; we shall be allowed to use our private keys to loose what doors of death we please.

GRATION: It was I who started talking of doors, but that gives you no right to make bad verse, with your "keys" and your "please." Moreover, Marcus, my dear, please do not use that word "gentleman" except in the conventional sense. We shall none of us be gentlemen after the event, and to tell you the honest truth (*he looks over his shoulder*), the Master himself is hardly a gentleman.

QUINTUS: No one ever thought him one. There are not many gentlemen in the army now. And as for the Command-in-Chief, the Service simply wouldn't tolerate a gentleman. They had enough of that under the progeny of Venus. [*All laugh except* MARCUS.]

PERTINAX: Yes, Marcus, Gration is right—I am sorry to say. You use that word "gentleman" too often. It doesn't matter to people like me, but the others are more sensitive.

MARCUS: (*abruptly*) Quintus, do you like this wine?

QUINTUS: No.

PERTINAX: (*warmly*) Don't listen to him, Marcus, it's simply his affectation and contrariness. The wine is excellent. It is the best I ever drank. (*He jerks three drops into the sand round the fountain-pool of the room.*) And I offer that to the gods below.

MARCUS: Are there then gods below the earth?

GRATION: Undoubtedly.

PERTINAX: So also the poets say. That is why I thought I would give those gods a little wine, since it seems they are athirst.

MARCUS: (*with subdued passion*) And do they receive the young, and the well-formed, and those that were lately full of life, and had before them gardens and good companions and women of their own kind to uphold them and to be upholden, and great views over the sacred land, and colonnades?

PERTINAX: And do they receive poor draggle-tailed debtors, who have been cuffed from table to table, and slink about between despairs, and . . .

MARCUS: Pertinax, Pertinax, will you approach such great things in so small a mood?

GRATION: You say "Great Things," great Marcus. You who are our leader in this affair, and of whom we are not ashamed, and with whom we go in company to seek that shady plain whence there is no return towards the things we loved. You say "Great Things." What know we of them? Even Socrates . . .

PERTINAX: Socrates again, with his snub nose! But I say, Socrates be . . .

MARCUS: (*interrupting him*) I have heard (and I despise them) those who have called it a transition towards unimaginable glories. But for my part, I have held it that death is nothing but a mighty sleep.

PERTINAX: Why then, if death is a mighty sleep, I would take a little nap. And you, Marcus, I know, will excuse me. For I never pretended to the manners of the gentry. You know how I hated dressing, and I cannot bear late hours. Treat me roughly if I snore. But if I do not snore, why, wake me when the military gentleman shall arrive. (*He wraps himself up in his cloak and lies down to sleep.*)

GRATION: I wonder how the hours now turn towards the dawn. . . . At first I thought I would ask your leave, Marcus, to go out awhile before the portico, beyond your rose trees, and there to put up my palms towards the skies and in prayer give my good-bye to the stars.

QUINTUS: No, Gration, stay here. Let us all be together, and continue in our conversation; for words interchanged are the support of souls, and it behoves men to do all great business in company. Now what greater business is there (*his voice rises somewhat, but gravely*) than to do what can be done for the State, and in failing, nobly to die?

MARCUS: (*after a pause*) You are right, Quintus; both in what you say of companionship, and in what you say of our endeavour. For though our enterprise seemed to many foolhardy, and even to very many more, self-seeking, at heart we loved the Republic, as fully did some in those days which, with my love of lineage, I have recalled. Nor is our work all wasted. Some fruit must come. Where and how we know not. (*Another pause.*) The eldest of us is not thirty. Yet we have done our work. Is not that glorious?

> [*There is a distant call without. Then a confused noise; then the distinct sound of rhythmical marching, a word of command, and the grounding of arms. All this some way off, in the night, beyond the garden, on the road.*]

GRATION: (*looking slowly at* MARCUS) I am ready, dear Marcus.

QUINTUS: And I.

> [*A* SLAVE *enters. He is an elderly, handsome man, with a fine grey beard, and nearly bald.*]

THE SLAVE: Noble Marcus, . . .

MARCUS: (*nodding*) I know what it is about, Fidelis. These are the times when men drink together. (*He hands him the cup.*)

THE SLAVE: (*bowing*) Sir, so I drank with your father.

MARCUS: And so you shall with my son. I have seen the lawyers, and you will be free, Fidelis. My mother will see to it. Show the officer in.

> [THE SLAVE *goes out, pulls back the curtain and announces* THE CENTURION.]

[The Centurion *salutes, pulls a little square thing from under his coat, and reads.*]

Centurion: (*after clearing his throat*) My orders are, sir, . . .

Marcus: (*to* The Centurion *with great courtesy*) Excuse me, Centurion; (*turning to* Quintus) shove Pertinax!

[Quintus *gives* Pertinax *a dig.* Pertinax *wakes up, gasping.*]

Pertinax: Eh? What? God dammit! Can't you let a fellow . . . ? Oh, I see. . . . I'm sorry. [*Nods at* The Centurion. *Stands up sleepily, watching the others all on their feet, and listening.*]

The Centurion: (*reading*) The Commander-in-Chief, sir, presents his compliments and hopes it will be convenient for you and these gentlemen to leave within one hour of sunrise and report at the Three Taverns at the second milestone outside the wall, where you shall receive orders for exile to your various estates. [*Mild sensation.* Marcus *completely suppresses a huge sigh of relief.* Quintus *remains impassive.* Gration *smiles as though he had expected reprieve all along.* The Centurion *continues.*] Any one of you may take as companion any other, so only that you report upon arrival. The Commander-in-Chief hopes that it will be convenient to you to remain in the country until his own return to Rome from the South. This will not be till the beginning of October. But he hopes that you will then call again at the Palatine, and that the former relations between him and yourselves may be resumed.

[The Centurion *salutes and prepares for a right-about turn.*]

209

Marcus: Will you not drink wine with me, Centurion?

Centurion: Why, sir, you're very kind, sir, I'm sure, sir.

[*He drinks.*]

Here's to you, sir, and all the other gentlemen.

Pertinax: Marcus, Marcus, I haven't got any wine. Give me some wine. [Marcus *hands him the cup.* Pertinax *turns gravely to* The Centurion] Here's to you! Very glad to have met you! Very glad indeed! Gladder than I thought I should be.

[The Centurion *salutes, turns stiffly, and goes out.*]

Marcus: The night is accomplished.

Pertinax: No, that's just what it isn't. Now, Marcus, who goes home with who?

XXXVII

Study of a *Mule*

WERE I in tune with my time (which I thank God I am not) I ought to call this "psycho-analysis of a mule." I won't give it any such title for a hundred reasons, among which are these: that the mule has no *psyche*; that if he had, it would be impossible to analyse it, for one cannot analyse a *psyche*; that the whole term "psycho-analysis" is charlatan; most of all that the mule could not speak, so that there was no getting at the recesses of his mind. Mules speak even less than donkeys. They are singularly dumb.

But I studied my mule and thought about him a great deal. Also I was grateful to him. Indeed I had thought of "Profession of Gratitude to a Mule" as a title for this, but there again that would have been an ill-judged phrase, for you can only be grateful to a rational being; you cannot be grateful to an animal any more than you can be just to an animal or respect the rights of an animal. I recommend this thought to all the subscribers to all the societies which promote gratitude, justice and worship in the matter of animals.

This very honest mule was introduced to me in a village of the Apennines a few weeks ago. He was but one of seven mules who stood all in a string patiently awaiting their burdens, of whom I was one; but I called him a predestined mule, a mule written down for honour, a mule apart and singular—for the burden he had to carry was me.

Another mule carried my bag: a little bag weighing nothing to speak of. When mules have heavy burdens to carry they hint at the magnitude of their task. They puff and blow and halt and wag their heads and show in general that they are the most magnanimous of beasts to consent to such enormous labour. They do exactly the same thing when they have nothing to carry. The other five mules were carrying empty sacks which, in the heights of the hills, were to be filled with charcoal. Yet they also put on a patient air, as who should say: "I have my duty to do and I do it. It will kill me, but I shall die in harness."

Slowly we went up in file by the rough path which zigzagged higher and higher, breasting the mountain-side. We were very many miles from any railway. A few years ago we should have been many miles from any machinery, or haste, or other ungracious thing. But to-day the internal combustion engine has come to destroy the world, and along the main road of the valley motor buses serve what were so very lately holy and secluded shrines. Anyhow, the people are not yet corrupt, but gentle and manly. Such were the muleteers, the two of them who conducted this long train. We had very soon left the valley road so far behind that we need think of it no more.

My mule, as he approached the highland solitudes, showed great indifference to the beauties of this world.

I have noticed in a life of much travel through places of great beauty that this is common to all animals and many men. Animals cannot laugh and they do not know the difference between right and wrong, and of beauty they have no idea. My mule went up into those divine hills with its head downwards and its eyes fixed upon the ground. I cannot blame him in this, for he had to pick his way very carefully from one stone to another, and he was very sure-footed, which virtue is of the essence of mules. There would be no point in being a mule at all if one were not sure-footed: and that is a lesson to us all: meaning, stick to your own talent, and, whatever you can do well, do it as well as you can, even if it be no more than lyric verse or architecture.

My mule also had this character about him, that he was reasonably stubborn in order to fulfil the Scripture, but he kept this less pleasing quality within bounds. In this again I found a lesson, for I said to myself; "This mule shows us how we ought to go all lengths in our good qualities—as, in sure-footedness—but to be re-strained in our less pleasant ones. So a taciturn man of good judgment will do well to excel in good judgment to the utmost, but let him beware of being too taciturn." My mule was stubborn in refusing hints from the muleteer to take short cuts that were too steep or to go too fast; also when he wanted to rest for a minute he would rest in spite of oaths. He knew his own business. But he was a manful mule, if I may so express myself; he never threatened to resign his task.

So we went upwards and upwards, mile after mile, over those deserted and splendid hills. With every pass-ing quarter of an hour the landscape increased. The

213

profound valleys, wherein lay the torrents and springs of those rivers which, when they reach the plains of Italy, are famous in the story of the world (Trebbia, Parma), fell into shadow under the afternoon sun, and there were apparent only upon every side the high rounded summits which, in this climate, are tree-clad throughout; even some thousands of feet above the sea.

My mule took no more notice of the gracious trees than of the vision of this world. He continued to perform his task. He held communion with none. He plodded. He bore his burden, and very glad I was he did so; but for his dutifulness I could never have reached the ridge and come down to the evening repose upon the farther side.

Time was, I would have walked across that divide with the best of them—indeed not so long ago; but the years work their will at last, and here was I now doing it, not on my human feet, but dependent upon a mule. That I should be so dependent made me ashamed, and I began writing verses in my head to commemorate my sadness at this decline. There were four verses. In one of them I made "mule" rhyme with "you'll." In another with "renewal." In another with "fuel," and in another with "pule"—which means to whine and be discontented—a verb long out of use. These verses I shall not publish for a long time, for I think that verse should be polished and repolished year after year, until the writer is as nearly satisfied as he can be—which is not saying much.

I think my mule wrote no verse. One cannot be certain. There was a banker not so long ago wrote admirable verse. Indeed there is nothing so unexpected as the Muse. But my mule showed not the least sign of verse writing, of which the most obvious sign is vanity. My mule was wholly without vanity. I say it to his praise.

We came upon the summit to a grove inhabited by the gods. I believe my mule knew well that the gods were there; inferior local gods, honest gods of the hills. I am sure that he was in communion with the spirits of the place and that they did not fill him with the novelty of emotion wherewith I was filled. For as for me, there was glory all around. The slanting sun, falling into the Mediterranean far away, had cast a very wide spell over all the leagues of highland. The colours were changing, and those things which men seek or imitate in the furniture of their lives (crimson and amethyst and gold and the translucence of thin airs and gems) were called up by the creative light throughout all the circle of that tumbled, but majestic horizon. It was as though the Italian mountains had put on a festival garment for the approaching evening. But my mule cared for none of these things. He began his downward way.

It was much steeper than the long climb had been. It was a descent through increasing shadows towards the villages far below, whence wood smoke was rising, and into a vineyard land. It grew darker, but not yet dark, as we went downwards. Then at last we came to water again, and the noise of man, and there it was that my mule and I came into a fellowship, and were agreed and thought of the same consummations. I had revered him as a strong and faithful servant, and I had felt gratitude to him as a helper, but now he became my brother for the first time. We were at one in our eagerness for the stable; good food and rest and litter (which only means a bed) and oblivion and the preparation for another day.

The last of the light fell as we reached the village in the dale, crossed the very high arched bridge of very ancient stone, and heard the bell from the tall fine tower of the church and saw the lights of habitations of man and mule-kind. There it was that, as I dismounted in the market-place with the first stars beginning to show in the liquid sky, I heard my mule sigh profoundly, and realised that in his heart he was saying: "That's all over. Now for bed." I hope he said his prayers; but I doubt it.

★ XXXVIII ★

On the Reputation of a Poet

THERE is a passage in *Alice in Wonderland* which I am never tired of quoting. When men get to a certain age they necessarily quote too often; so I must beg my readers to forgive me if I have alluded to that passage before in other books. It is worthy of continual reference, for it illustrates the very heart of clear thinking.

Alice is talking to the White Knight about a song of his, and when he tells her the name of it, she says, "So that is the song?" But he tells her that she is quite mistaken. It is not the song; it is only the name of the song. When she suggests that that is what the song is called, he gets testy, and tells her it is called nothing of the kind. The *name* of the song is one thing; what it is *called* is another. And so forth.

In parallel with this I would beg to point my finger at the title I have written above. I am inquiring curiously upon what makes or hinders the reputation of a poet: not on what makes him a poet, or hinders him from being one—which is quite another matter; nor what helps him or prevents him from writing poetry— which is a third and totally distinct thing.

I am concerned to consider this little matter for two

217

very different reasons. The first of these reasons is that poetry is the highest kind of writing. Now, since nations are great through their writers, they will be especially great through their poets. As I am being so finicky, by the way, I ought to write, not "through their poets," but "through the reputation of their poets"; as, for instance, of Isaiah (the first of that limited company), of Sophocles (better known to one sacred band as Bophocles), and of Camoens—of whom neither you nor I have ever read a word. But a State or nation might be as big as America and remain nothing to history if its poets either were not, or did not survive. I beg your pardon—I mean, if the reputation of its poets did not exist and survive.

The first question I have to ask (and I do not propose to answer any certainly save the two last) is, whether bulk of poems be a necessary element in the greatness of a poet? Clearly, bulk alone will not suffice; but can a man be a great poet, or have the reputation of one, if he writes but little?

Here we have a question of degree. No one will call a poet a great poet because he has written only one very good couplet or single line. Manifestly, a poet who can turn out masses of first-rate stuff, like Victor Hugo, is the greater for his bulk. But where are we to draw the line? Will anyone deny that Theocritus was a great poet, or Catullus? I have heard Gray disputed. I would not dispute him.

But here we must beware of confounding enthusiasm for beauty with a reputation for poetry. Because a few of us swear by the writer of a few things, it does not follow that many men will do so. And it is the many (though generally instructed by the few) who, spread over long time, are the makers of reputation. An intense admiration of some few short things is not sufficient for reputation; there must be a general appreciation, diffused, and permanent. But I incline (though I positively answer none of these questions) to the judgment that one should draw the line well to the left. Bulk is of much less importance than the men of our time (who have gone idiotically wrong in substituting numbers for value) would generally concede.

Next, I would ask whether the reputation of a poet is marred or destroyed by the inclusion under his name of a great mass of bad verse? Here the probable reply would seem to be that no amount of bad verse will destroy a sufficient, though very small nucleus of good verse; and that the good verse floats the bad, as corks float a net. I make that reply for the general, not for myself. It has always seemed to me (but it is only a personal opinion) that a man of so detestably false a taste as to include very much bad verse with his good verse cannot at heart be a poet; and therefore ought not to have the reputation of one. His true reputation should be "John Smith, a detestably bad poet, stumbled upon a few good lines." Or, again, "John Smith, a vile poet during most of his life, wrote well during a bare five years of his life." In the first category some would put Longfellow; in the second, Wordsworth. But don't go about saying I did so.

The general, the masses, the herd, once they are told that a man has written really good verse, will excuse any amount of bad verse attached to his name.

I next approach a point on which all tradition is in

219

my favour and all the modern hullabaloo is against me. Can change in popular mood destroy permanently the reputation of a good poet? All the modern hullabaloo would answer, Yes. All tradition would answer, No. You must give the wind time to blow a man down. He will bow to it, and bow flat; but if the wind of time does not uproot him, his reputation will re-erect itself. There is something permanent in the judgment of man which is a reflection, though a pale and distorted one, of that permanent good whereupon the universe reposes. But the converse point, whether reputation may not be artificially supported by elements non-poetical, and whether in the disappearance of these the reputation will not crash, may be answered differently (I hope) and in a fashion more satisfactory to the dignity of the human mind. Bad verse does lose its false glory with a change in the public mood.

Of factitious supports for reputations, I know none more powerful nor more despicable than the religious spirit, whether in connection with the highest idea of the Divine or with the lowest (as a fetish), or with something in between (such as patriotism). There was a famous repartee in my youth given to a man who asked a critic to praise him for his verse. The critic answered doubtfully, "I do not know if it will stand alone; but at any rate you should have it set to music."

Now verse which depends for its appeal upon an emotion not poetic is a borrower under the basest conditions of borrowing, and time, I take it, will winnow out that chaff ruthlessly. (But I write under correction.) This is not to say, as do some fools, that verse inspired by patriotism or any other religion will necessarily be bad. Witness the Song of Deborah and, if you will allow me to mention them, the noble rhetorical odes of Campbell. I often muse with pleasure upon the memory that, amid all the base worms upon whom public money was showered in the Napoleonic wars, this poet got some of it. To-day he would get nothing, unless he had made a good contract with his publishers.

Lastly, let me ask these two questions. First: Can a man have the reputation of a poet who is publicly known for some other craft than letters, e.g. a politician, a soldier, a crook?

I answer "No." To have the reputation of a poet you must keep off everything else and starve.

Next, I ask: Does the reputation of a poet decline with a decline in the reading of him, or even of a bare acquaintance with the tongue in which he wrote?

Here I can give a very certain answer: it does not. I have myself with my own ears heard a London taxi-driver say to another (who perhaps had wandered into popular verse), "You think you're a pocket Homer, don't you?" (If I do not reproduce the accent it is because I do not know how to do it.) Many an English gentleman regards Corneille as a great poet, though actually despising the French language, and certainly ignorant of Corneille. I myself, who have not a word of German, revere the names of Heine and of Goethe; and I could fancy that if a good translation and a proper boom were to make some Chinese poet enduringly famous, then that Chinese poet would achieve enduring fame, though all who praised him were blindly ignorant of his idiom. Indeed, which of us to-day has any idea how classical Greek was pronounced? Yet pronunciation is the essence of poetry, for poetry resides in the magic of sound and the association of words.

The conclusion of the matter is this. If we could come back to earth eleven hundred years hence (I allow about eleven hundred years at the most for the swamping of good stuff and its reappearance on the surface— as, for instance, A.D. 350—A.D. 1450), we should find the old names standing. And what about the modern names? I will tell you all about them when we meet again in three hundred years.

★ XXXIX ★

The Place of Peace

PEOPLE are always talking about peace in these days, and they will probably go on talking about it until some fighting begins again somewhere, and then they will talk of it more shrilly than ever; for the acute necessity of it will be even more apparent than it is now.

Well, while they have been talking about it, I have found it. I did not find it to keep, for that is impossible; but I found it to hold for a few days, and it is a great deal to be able to say even that.

I found it cleverly (though I say it that should not) and by a deliberate plan—which is a very rare way of finding anything good. For good things from outside usually come upon one as gifts from others—among whom I include Providence. We do not usually ferret them out for ourselves. So true is this that I, who have known the Cathedral of Chartres intimately for forty years, stumbled for the first time the other day upon one particular statue in the Adoration of the Magi which I had never known to exist, and which I at once had photographed, because it was the most beautiful thing I had ever seen in my life: far, far superior to the basso-relievos upon the London offices of the Metropolitan Railway.

Well, as I was saying, I found peace of set purpose and by plan. I have in my house the detailed maps of a good many European countries, as well as of England. I looked up a mountainous part of one of these countries, and carefully scanned the features of several sections in it, in order to choose out the most promising. I made my selection among a dozen or more secluded valleys, giving preference to those which had woods about them, and wholly excluding all which were approached by a railway, however light and frivolous, and even those which were traversed by a main road; for petrol has become a worse curse than ever railways were, and I often wonder what old Ruskin would say if he could come to life. Seeing that he had already exhausted his vocabulary against railways, I suppose that against petrol he would have nothing left but gesticulation.

I took care, of course, that the district should lie in the older culture of Europe, for those that lie in the newer culture, that is, those that have lost the Faith, are not made for repose.

You might think it impossible to find such a place, but I found it, marked with its few houses, and its Church; and I set out to reach it: two easy days and nights from London, and the last few miles by a path, on foot.

While I was still in the forest, it being late morning, misgivings began to overtake me, as they will some hours after one's last meal, and I wondered whether there would be an inn at all, and if there were, whether it would be pleasing, and especially whether the people who kept it would be kind and hospitable (for that is the principal good about an inn, and its absence the principal evil); whether the wine would be potable, whether there would be an absence of buzz-saws or other worse instruments of the modern mountain-side. Then one of those horrible black thoughts which come swooping on one from nowhere like an evil bird struck me sideways. What about wireless?

But when the forest ended and I saw before me the steep and ancient roofs, the strong grey dignified stone walls, and the tiny church of the little place, I was already relieved. A slope of sweet meadow ran down to it from the ends of the wood, (which stopped short all along, like a low cliff). On the grass cows wandered about, occupied in eating and in making a heavenly music with bells, which is the only instrument a cow can play—but she plays it divinely well. The path led on through this sward, and I came into the village and found the inn.

Then there began that discovery; and it was so good that with difficulty could I believe that it was real; or at any rate, if it were real, hardly of this ruined world. The inn was called "The Green Cross," and I found at a table in the large front room a handsome elderly woman peeling potatoes. As the Latin poet says of the good woman, "she kept to her own house and she carded wool." Only his Good Woman was not dealing with wool, but with potatoes, which had not in the Latin poet's time been brought over the Atlantic seas, with many other modern good and evil things. She rapidly displayed all the virtues inherent to her race, sex, age, and the rest of it. She was kind, she was sensible, she knew what her prices were (six shillings and fivepence English a day, with wine—I had taken the precaution to drink some of the wine to begin with, before saying that I wanted to stop there—it was quite good wine; not as good as she was, nor as good as the common wine of Orange on the Rhone, whence came the title of the detestable family, but still a great deal better than the stuff you pay seven or eight shillings for in London— and this wine was thrown in, not charged for, offered liberally, like water or air or sunshine, as wine was intended to be, only, as you may remember, things went wrong within a few hours after sunrise upon the last day of Creation: this sentence, and digression, are between them getting too long; so I close the bracket, and end the sentence: but before doing so, I cannot refrain from remarking that all the discussions of the silly critics as to whether sentences in English should be long or short are mere spoiling of paper), and she took me to a room of immense size with thick walls, heavy curtains, a washed plank floor, an admirable bed at least three generations old, and a window opening on to the sublime hills.

Therein lay peace. The core of it was in that room. Old Sleep inhabited it by night, and by day the air of the mountains, and by day and by night the noise of the running water in the dale.

For three days I inhabited this place, reading the life of Bossuet, which I had brought with me, and writing a little verse, and often wandering to the small waterfalls and tarns in the uplands of that country-side. But on the fourth day I thought I would be gone. One should not tempt such things, or abuse the gift of them. If too great beauty and too great intelligence are dangerous, and certainly too great wealth, and even perhaps too great bodily well-being, then blessed Peace must not be over-indulged. And I thought to myself as I went off down the valley by the rough road, behind an old horse (for there was no car in the place), that I had done well not to linger longer, like the lady in the song. I looked back over my shoulder at the tiny village, but I did not give it any benediction, for that would have been superfluous.

You ask me where it was, that you may go and enjoy it yourself? But I have come to the end of my book, and so I have no room left in which to tell you this.

THE END